The Diary of Gull Mohammad

The Diary of Gull Mohammad

A Kashmiri Muslim boy's journey from Kashmir to Kerala

HUMRA QURAISHI

OXFORD
UNIVERSITY PRESS

OXFORD
UNIVERSITY PRESS

Oxford University Press is a department of the University of Oxford.
It furthers the University's objective of excellence in research, scholarship,
and education by publishing worldwide. Oxford is a registered trade mark of
Oxford University Press in the UK and in certain other countries

Published in India by
Oxford University Press
22 Workspace, 2nd Floor, 1/22 Asaf Ali Road, New Delhi 110002, India

© Oxford University Press India 2023

First Edition published in 2023

The moral rights of the author have been asserted

ISBN-13 (print edition): 978-9-39-105026-9
ISBN-10 (print edition): 9-39-105026-3

ISBN-13 (eBook): 978-9-35-497298-0
ISBN-10 (eBook): 9-35-497298-5

ISBN-13 (oso): 978-9-35-497304-8
ISBN-10 (oso): 9-35-497304-3

DOI: 10.1093/oso/9789391050269.001.0001

Typeset in Minion Pro 10.5/14
by Newgen Knowledge Works Pvt. Ltd.
Printed and bound in India by Replika Press Pvt. Ltd.

This Diary is for my grandchildren—Ali and Hasan and Amna. And also for Mohammad Fareed, the little boy I had met over four years back in a New Delhi-situated madrasa; his sharp-featured face with those emotion-dripping eyes stand out to this day. And for all the children I have been meeting in the various madrasas all these years.

Contents

Acknowledgements

I have quoted the verses of Kashmir's sufis and poets and also all the other verses in this 'Diary', from the two volumes titled—'Kashir—Being a History of Kashmir from the Earliest Times to Our Own' (Capital Publishing House, New Delhi)—by the well-known historian, G.M.D Sufi. In fact, these two well-researched and well-written volumes focus on just about every aspect to Kashmir and to the Kashmiris. A must read for researchers, students, and also for writers! Though historian G.M.D. Sufi passed away decades back but he is remembered to this day for his historical works. I have his two volumes with me, placed high up on the book shelf. I have been reading them for years and even quote from them. Indeed, I'm grateful to historian Sufi.

And regarding the inputs to the Kashmir situated Sufi dargahs and shrines of these sufis, I have been travelling to these dargahs and shrines. All these years I have been writing on their historical significance and philosophy and architecture. I have visited each one of these dargahs and shrines, several times, if not many times. And read details to them in the above mentioned two volumes by G.M.D. Sufi and also in the books written by other historians.

Also, I'm thankful to all the Kashmiris who have been sharing their experiences . . . I have been travelling to the Kashmir Valley right from 1990 and I have been reporting and writing extensively on the situation and its impact on the Kashmiris. I have held creative writing workshops for the students in the Universities situated in the Kashmir Valley. And have heard some very painful accounts from the young and also from members of the APDP (Association of Parents of Disappeared Persons) whose children have been picked up by security agencies for questioning and never got back! The young Kashmiris are angry and restless. After all, all that they have witnessed in the last several years is bloodshed, killings, curfews, and crackdowns. And they are also well aware of the historical facts to the Kashmir Valley and also what's been happening around, in the subcontinent and in the rest of the world.

I'm extremely thankful to the entire team at the Oxford University Press (OUP) for publishing this Diary. I'm also thankful to Praveena of Newgen for her fine editing and patience.

Introduction

The Diary of Gull Mohammad—A Kashmiri Muslim boy's journey from Kashmir to Kerala

As I sit and begin to write this Introduction to the diary of a 14-year-old Kashmiri boy, Gull Mohammad —who, because of the prevailing ground realities in the Kashmir Valley, is shifted by his parents from their home in Srinagar's downtown, to a madrasa in New Delhi and then confronted with further twists and turns in his life—faces of hundreds of innocent children do stand out.

For the last over three decades, I have been visiting orphanages and madrasas in the towns and cities I travel to. Even while residing in New Delhi and, later in the suburbs/NCR, I have been visiting madrasas rather too regularly. With that, interacting with the children—the so-called madrasa children—and also with the maulvis, though, it's only occasionally that I could get to meet the children's parents or grandparents. Many of these children are orphans or semi-orphans (one of the parents was dead), but even those whose parents are alive seem to be living cut off, because their parents are seemingly in no position financially, to keep travelling to meet them. I got the impression that a large number of these children have been sent to madrasas so that they get two square meals a day and perhaps have a 'safe' roof over their heads.

These visits to the madrasas got me close to the realities in which these children are surviving in. Not to overlook a vital factor—as a majority of these madrasas do not have televisions sets nor radios, nor any of the modern-day connecting gadgets, so the traditional living conditions are intact and with that the innocence to these madrasa children. Their stark innocence, raw emotions, that forlorn look in their eyes has left an imprint. It is difficult to describe that look of helplessness in their eyes and body language, and together with that my own dilemma of how to reach out to them. After all, my visits to these madrasas have been somewhat

The Diary of Gull Mohammad. Humra Quraishi, Oxford University Press. © Oxford University Press India 2023.
DOI: 10.1093/oso/9789391050269.003.0001

brief. Though each time I'm tempted to stay back longer but as a woman I have got to adhere to the supposed don'ts!

Traditionally, single and unescorted women walking into boys' madrasas is not the done thing. It is not accepted, nor expected! And if women do go ahead and walk into the confines of a boys' madrasa with rations or food, they are not expected to linger around for long.

During my visits, I sat talking to the children and the maulvis about their daily routine; what they ate, what they read, and also about their families and ancestral setups back home. With that I could manage to grasp backgrounders to them. Most of the children came across as shy and subdued and didn't talk much, but their eyes carried varying emotions. . . relayed much. A large number of them lacked confidence to such an extent that they couldn't talk beyond a word or a sentence or two. Needless to add, their body language relayed nervousness and anxiety.

My madrasa visits have been emotionally fulfilling for me. I developed a bonding and connect with these children. So much so, that if I wasn't a writer (i.e., surviving as a full-time writer!), I would have been only too happy and relaxed manning a madrasa and looking after the madrasa children! Yes, that would have been the case, because by now I have seen too much of the worldly people and have been left totally disillusioned by the layers around them. I'm completely put off by the fake and synthetic settings to the so-called who's who of today's India.

In contrast stand out the ground realities of the madrasas and the innocence of the children housed in there. Of course, the conditions of the madrasas and also of the Muslim orphanages differ from region to region.

Several children's 'homes' situated in the Kashmir Valley (where orphaned and even semi-orphaned children are lodged), are comparatively better than most of the madrasas I have visited in and around New Delhi, Uttar Pradesh, and in Haryana's Mewat belt. In these madrasas, it's just the sheer basics to the daily survival that stood out.

It came as a pleasant surprise to see many of the Kashmir Valley-situated orphanages, follow a 'via media' between a madrasa and the regular mainstream education—in the sense, the children attend a regular school but in the evenings and early mornings (i.e., after attending school and before setting off for school), they read the Quran and tend to other religious texts.

This, according to me, is the best possible combination, but for obvious reasons not quite affordable. Not to overlook the fact that unlike in the Mughal era or even in later decades when the Zamindari system was not demolished and abolished, madrasa teaching was funded and taken care of by this ruling class; today, the madrasas are maintained on meagre resources, mainly put together by the community members or at times by the waqf boards. In fact, today the children brought to the madrasas by their relatives are from the economically deprived and socially disadvantaged families. As I have earlier mentioned it wouldn't be amiss to say that many of these children could have been sent to the madrasas for the very basics—food and safe shelter.

Interestingly, until 1970s, or perhaps even until 1980s, the middle class did enrol their children for madrasa education and did so with great pride and confidence. Many professionals I have come across, told me that for their early education, they attended the madrasas in their towns or cities and qasbahs.

One of my former colleagues at the Academy of Third World Studies (Jamia Millia Islamia, New Delhi, where I was a Visiting Professor), Dr. Nasir Raza Khan, told me that until class eight, he had studied in his home town-situated madrasa, Niazia Nizamia, in Bihar. With English not as the medium of instruction in madrasas, how did he cope with further studies, and also what about those talks that fundamentalism holds sway in madrasas? 'Yes, English was not taught . . . and till class eight I didn't know many of the elementary English words but that didn't make me feel disadvantaged. Later I picked up the English language; it required a lot of hard work but I managed. . . Today Muslims are going through tough times because of the "thappa" (blot) thrown at them by vested interests that Islam is radical, but those are all false stories only to defame the community'. And I was rather surprised to hear the New Delhi-based lawyer, M.R. Shamshad, tell me that he and his siblings did their schooling in a madrasa in Bihar. Today, he comes across as though he had a public school background to him.

Also, much against the popular perception that only Muslim families send their children to study in a madrasa, the fact is that this wasn't always the case. In the traditional setups, when communal poisoning was not unleashed to divide and distance, even non-Muslim families sent their children to madrasas for education. In fact, several years back, in 2006,

I had come across this feature in the Outlook magazine, and I found it so very laden with off-beat facts that I kept it safely with me all these years.

This feature by Jaideep Mazumdar could be an eye-opener for madrasa-bashers. He wrote—'The Bengal Alifate—Going to the madrasa here in like studying in any other school. Proof: Hindu students . . . why the state's madrasas are special—Some 40,000 Hindus -12% of total students- study in them. They are co-educational—in fact girls outnumber boys and sit in the same classroom as them. No mullahs teach here, there are several Hindus among the teachers. Save for a compulsory paper in either Arabic or Islamic Studies, the syllabi are the same as in any other secondary school of the state. The class X certificate is recognized by the state secondary board. They (madrasas) are popular with Hindus as the fee is minimal, the teacher student ratio is 42:1, quality of education is often better. . . '

Realities of the Day

Madrasa children, the most vulnerable in the communally surcharged climate of today's India, are soft targets for the Hindutva goon brigades. Not just in the Bharatiya Janata Party (BJP) ruled states but also in the National capital, New Delhi! In 2018, an eight-year-old child, Mohammad Azeem, studying in a madrasa situated in the South Delhi's Begampur was lynched by the local goons.

Shockingly, this was not the first time that a madrasa child was targeted in that very locality of South Delhi. In 2017, a small group of madrasa children were brutally thrashed in a park, once again in the Begampur locality, by the Right-Wing goons after forcing them to chant Bharat Mata Ki Jai! And to compound the tragedy there wasn't a single reaction from any of the political setups, nor from the various commissions.

And in the summer of 2019, on 11 July, madrasa children were targeted in Uttar Pradesh's Unnao, with three of the children seriously injured. They were attacked with cricket bats and stumps and even stones pelted on them. According to the news reports, the imam of the Jama Masjid of Unnao stated that a group of men from the Bajrang Dal were involved in that attack on the madrasa children.

These madrasa children were attacked —— attacked when they were going to play cricket at the GIC grounds in Unnao. A group of men from the Right-Wing walked up to them and forced them to chant Jai Shri Ram. And when these children tried to flee, stones were pelted at them. 'Almost all of them (the madrasa children) had their kurtas ripped by the miscreants,' said Naeem Miswahi, the imam of the Darul Uloom Faizee Aam Madrasa in Unnao.

Though an FIR was lodged, no comments on this onslaught on the madrasa children from the Child Rights forums, nor from the Minority Commissions or the Ministry dealing with Women and Children.

Then, on 16 July 2019—national dailies carried details of a madrasa targeted in Uttar Pradesh. To quote from the news report in The National Herald—'Violence in UP Village. Madrasa set ablaze—Violence erupted in Behta village in Fatehpur district on Tuesday after animal flesh was found in the village near a pond. After residents claimed that cow slaughter had taken place in the village, and news spread, people from several villages collected and vandalised a madrasa and then set it on fire. Senior officials rushed to the village and additional police force was called in to control the situation.'

* * *

The truth is that madrasa children are most vulnerable in today's India where communalism has been so very systematically unleashed that 'Muslim-looking' children attired in kurta–pyjama with skull caps on, can be targeted by the well-trained Hindutva brigades. In fact, for the last several years, I have been visiting madrasas situated in various locales of the capital city, and what saddens me is that the madrasa children feel insecure stepping out to the nearby parks or the market places. If they do step out of the madrasa confines, then it is only in small groups. They confided that apprehensions do hold out, with the Hindutva brigades on the prowl to lynch and kill.

And to compound the situation, the community leaders and the so-called politically and socially influential persons from the Muslim community are seldom seen interacting with the madrasa children. Their presence is urgently needed; at least it would provide some level of cushioning, which is crucial for the very safety of the young children studying in the madrasas. I sit back and wonder, why the well-to-do Muslims are not reaching out to the madrasa children!

Also, not to overlook the fact that over the years the Right-Wing has managed to spread the most vicious propaganda against madrasas. And none of our politicians or even the community leaders have managed to counter any of this utterly bogus and vicious and third-rate propaganda.

Madrasa bashing seems to be the order of the day. Hear the speeches of the political mafia and they try and link any terror activity to madrasas! To link madrasas with terrorist activities has become a fashionable ploy to attack, if not, hound these children.

I have visited many madrasas. Mind you, each time with a critical eye and came back feeling depressed. Yes, very sad and forlorn. Seeing the bare basics with which the boys were living in. The madrasas in Haryana's Mewat and even the ones here in New Delhi are so basic that one felt as though entering an ancient setup—with no radios, no computers, and also no television sets. Maybe just an Urdu newspaper clutched in the maulvi's hands.

And on the several occasions when I visited the Lucknow-situated Nadwa (one of the most sought-after centres in India for Islamic religious studies), one felt as though transported to a Gandhian ashram. Clad in cotton kurta–pyjamas, young boys going about in that no-fuss manner, with the basic wooden furniture dotted in the rooms of this institution. There were only a few computers. And to the 'why' to few computers, the answer was that where are the funds for more, although the children seemed very keen to use computers. What about the talks that Nadwa gets grants and aid from several Muslim countries? The maulanas of Nadwa rubbished those reports and told me that it runs on whatever little the community can muster, including the *zakat* money, which Muslims give for the needy and disadvantaged.

I recall, asking the religious head of the Muslim community in the Kashmir Valley, Mirwaiz Umar Farooq, during the course of an interview, whether he was worried that various negatives get thrown at madrasas? And this is what he said:'On the pretext of terrorism these Right-Wing people are attacking madrasas ... it is part of the Hindutva brigade's agenda to spread all this disinformation.'

When I'd asked Milli Gazette's editor, Zafarul Islam Khan, why madrasas are getting linked to terrorism, he'd reacted—'when LK Advani used to say about madrasas being places of terrorist-activities, we not just wrote strongly countering this but even sent a team of 10 to 12 reporters to the Indo-Nepal border situated madrasas to see and study the situation for themselves . . . there was nothing . I have myself studied in a madrasa and there's nothing in madrasas except teaching - 60% is the teaching of the regular subjects like Hindi, English, Social studies, and about 40% is religious study. What's wrong with this!' And to the RightWing's allegations gaining ground, he'd said—'We have even proof that all those comments made by L. K. Advani are baseless. I'd even retorted to Tavleen Singh's write-up and had even asked her to come and study the madrasas before levelling all those charges but she didn't reply! What can one do to this sort of thing of flinging wild charges without any accountability.'

And the well-known commentator, the late Asghar Ali Engineer had also reacted rather strongly when I asked him to comment on Right-Wing's anti-madrasa propaganda—'This is nothing but propaganda! Who says our madrasas are teaching all this! I don't know of any such madrasa. If you ask about some particular madrasas in Pakistan, then they were setup and started by CIA, for a definite purpose!'

Several other academics also pointed out that the Right-Wing had not so long ago accused the Christian schools and missionaries of trying to convert students. 'Its along the same pattern that they are labelling these charges against the Muslim schools of learning. Where, mind you, even the non-Muslims have had the tradition of studying.'

* * *

And much in keeping with my visiting the various madrasas, I have been also keeping track of the various writings on madrasas. In fact, I had to read and then re-read the news report published in The Tribune (The Tribune—dated 22 August 2005). It was senior journalist Anita Katyal's front page report with this caption—Not a Single madrasa in Jammu and Kashmir. Kerala has 6,000, Uttar Pradesh, 4, 292. And along with this caption the rest of the report had this to state – ' Terrorists and jehadi groups, armed and trained in Pakistan run camps and madrasas, have been operating for several years in Jammu and Kashmir, the only Muslim majority state in India. And yet, for all the troubles in this border state, there is not a single madrasa in Jammu and Kashmir. In sharp contrast, Kerala, which is on the far end of the country is peaceful and free from terrorist activity. Yet it has 6000 madrasas, the largest number in India. Its shares this honour with Madhya Pradesh which has the same number of religious schools. Uttar Pradesh, which shares a long and porous border with Nepal, comes next having 4, 292 madrasas, whilst Bihar is next on the list with 4,102. Of the 27,000 odd officially linked madrasas Rajasthan has 1,985 and Gujarat 1727. The state wise breakup was made available in Parliament by the HRD Ministry. The functioning of madrasas has been in the spotlight after the 9/11 terrorist attack as right wing politicians have stepped up their charge that these institutions have been used by Pakistan's ISI to train and mobilize jehadi groups. This issue had figured in the parliament several times in recent years when BJP leaders pointed to the rapid spread of madrasas in border areas, saying that these are essentially centres of Islamic fundamentalists indulging in anti-national activities and therefore need to be watched. Going by this perception and given the scale of cross border terrorism in J&K, the state should have a wide network of such institutions. Yet, it has none . . . 'This is yet another example of how incorrectly J&K is perceived by the outside world', says Lok Sabha MP Mehbooba Mufti, who heads Jammu and Kashmir Peoples Democratic Party (PDP). Contrary to the popular belief, she said the people of Kashmir have never believed in fundamentalism, and the state is actually known for its culturssal composite character. 'The Islam practiced here is more moderate and has its basics in sufism', she explains. The PDP leader believes that the growth of madrasas is primarily linked to economic problems. She said that poor parents sent their children to these schools as they are imparted free education.' (end of Anita Katyal's report).

* * *

And though successive governments in the country have been coming with tall claims that they would be making madrasa-educated students get into the mainstream education, such proclamations often turn out to be somewhat hollow and bogus. To quote from The Tribune news report:

'Madrasa pupils fail to make it to JNU
Akhila Singh
Tribune News Service.
(Published on 15 August 2009)

14 August, New Delhi—Attempts by the government to allow students of madrasas (religious schools) to enrol at a mainstream university seem to have come to a nought. Jawaharlal Nehru University (JNU) had, for the first time, announced in its prospectus that starting from this academic session, certificates of selected madrasas would be treated at par with the regular school leaving (Class 12) diplomas.

However, university records show that not a single madrasa student has been able to clear JNU's entrance examination for undergraduate courses. The fact that the test was conducted in English probably might have been the reason.

Sources close to JNU said that the university held a common entrance test for all students seeking admission in the B.A. course, for which madrasa certificates were also deemed as valid.

JNU is the country's first varsity other than Jamia Millia Islamia and Aligarh Muslim University to have recognized certificates issued by madrasa for enrolment in undergraduate courses. The university prospectus lists 17 madrasas in Uttar Pradesh and Bihar, whose students can appear for the entrance tests of undergraduate courses in foreign languages. The move came less than three years after the Justice Rajinder Sachar Committee Report which recommended 'social and economic upliftment' of Muslims in India.

In the past, students with madrasa certificates used a circuitous route to study at JNU. They first enrolled in the B.A.-I course in Arabic at Jamia Millia Islamia, which recognizes madrasa certificates. Then, they moved to JNU for the second-year B.A. course. Besides Arabic and Persian, JNU runs undergraduate courses in other foreign languages also.

Former JNU Students Union president Dhananjay Tripathi said: 'Rules need to be changed even if it was a case of just one student being placed at a disadvantage. The Sachar panel's recommendations stated it was crucial for madrasa students to be brought into mainstream education'.

However, with no madrasa student clearing the JNU entrance test in English for undergraduate courses, the efforts seem wasted.' (end of the Tribune news report).

* * *

Till date, I haven't come across a Kashmiri Muslim child's diary, written in the English language. I have written this child's diary in the present context, in the ongoing political situation prevailing in the country. Going by the build-ups, this situation is worsening with the Right-Wing agenda accelerating. And the worst affected are the young. I have been travelling to the Kashmir Valley right from 1990, and I have been reporting and writing extensively on the situation and its impact on the Kashmiris. My earlier published books—*Kashmir: The Untold Story*, (2004, Penguin) and *Kashmir The Unending Tragedy: Reports from the Front Lines (2019, Amaryllis)*—carry details of the havoc. Also, in my novel—*Meer* (2015, Rupa)—I have tried to web-in the impact of the violence on the young Kashmiris.

It is significant to mention that in recent years, I have come across only one volume (in the English language) focusing on the madrasas for girls in the Indian context. And it is—Dr Hem Borker's—'Madrasas and the Making of Islamic Womanhood' (OUP), where she focuses on madrasas for girls. To the best of my knowledge, there is no other full-fledged volume in the English language focusing on the experience of living and learning in a madrasa in India. This itself is a sad commentary. After all, in the recent history of the country or for that matter of the subcontinent, madrasas were considered as the apt institutions for learning and knowledge. Till, of course, the ongoing Right-Wing propaganda, demolishing the very significance that ought to be given to these institutions. Madrasa critics don't even bother to enter a madrasa and see for themselves the exact realities. Unlike the phobia created, these madrasas are places where just about anyone can enter and talk and walk around. And with that, can get to see the day's happenings and grasp the actual realities.

Communally surcharged politics has heaped havoc to such an extent that every madrasa child or even a visitor to a madrasa is looked at with suspicion and disbelief and much more!

When I tell my friends that I prefer to spend my birthdays or any other day with the madrasa children, I get those strange looks of utter disbelief! As though relaying I'm indulging in some hopelessly bizarre or outdated, if not dangerous activity!

* * *

The prime purpose to put together this diary is to try relay what a madrasa child has to go through in these communally surcharged times. This diary written over a period of approximately just over a year, from early

August 2016 till about the second week of September 2017, is enough to relay the tough, challenging times these children face.

Today there is an ongoing onslaught on young psyches. Though this has been on for several years, earlier it was more along the subtle format but now out there, blatantly aggressive. Yet we don't seem to be reacting! I wonder why! Either we have become thick-skinned or brutally insensitive to the ground realities.

I have purposely focused on the boys' madrasas because in my view in today's India and the general political climate, a Muslim male is at a more disadvantaged position that the Muslim female. I had first noticed this in the Kashmir Valley where boys and young men faced the brunt of State-unleashed terror on the roads and highways. I've seen young boys accompanying me, getting frisked and pushed around by the security men in the most humiliating ways. Many of them stood hunched in that hopeless forlorn way.

And in these recent years, the same patterns are emerging in the rest of the country. Lynch victims happen to be Muslim men and their sons. They also happen to be victims of discrimination where jobs and livelihoods and housing are concerned. Not to overlook the other unsettling fact—the percentage of the jailed Muslim men is much higher in proportion to the Muslim population in India. I wonder why?

In recent years, Muslim boys and young men have been telling me that they are very apprehensive of their very survival—their future, in terms of their safety and upkeep and livelihood. What, with pracharacks and maha-pracharacks ruling, and their private senas calling the shots!

* * *

This manuscript, written as a Diary, focuses on the ground realities. Names and surnames of the men, women and children, mentioned in this Diary have been changed; their identity protected, for their safety and privacy. Also, webbed and inter-webbed are several fictional factors-connectors-characters too.

1

Shifting from Srinagar

2 August 2016—8 a.m.

This drizzle! Want to somehow sneak out, towards the inner lanes, towards the *Badam Wari* (almond orchard), around the almond trees growing around the dargah of Makhdoom sahib. And just sit there in peace! No peace here . . . feeling suffocated! Gulzar's coughing . . . ongoing, not stopping. He could have wrapped all the leftover shawls lying stacked all over this room! What else, with no sales all these summer months. Gulzar unmoving like these shawls! What's going wrong with him, doesn't listen. Look even now sitting like a statue, peeping out of the window. What's there to see outside—only stray dogs and these police fellows loitering around with those guns in their hands! Hate all this . . . these creatures stationed on our heads . . . don't know how many more of us will get killed by these creatures . . . when this curfew getting lifted!

Why wasn't anyone not telling me of Meer Khandey's killing in last night's firing? Don't they know I'm stronger than Gulzar but they treat me as though I'll have a breakdown. I didn't even cry when Bilal was gunned down right across the lane. I'm fourteen but my brain is that of a twenty-year old. Though my mouj (mother) treats me as though I'm some new born!

9 a.m.

Surely toth (father) is not getting ready to attend Meer Khandey's janaza . . . doesn't he realize that *pondeh police* (Kashmiri slang for cops), will pull him by the collar. Saw Bilal's father slapped and dragged when he was carrying his son's dead body . . . can't get over the way these devils were kicking the auto rickshaw carrying Bilal's bleeding dead form!

11 a.m.

This Gulzar's stubbornness! Not moving from the window. Didn't even let me close the window till the pellet shells hit the glass panes. No money

The Diary of Gull Mohammad. Humra Quraishi, Oxford University Press. © Oxford University Press India 2023.
DOI: 10.1093/oso/9789391050269.003.0002

for any of the new glass repairs. Now more breeze hitting his chest but wouldn't move from the window. I know his cough isn't going to get any better. No kehwah left . . . all the shops shut here. First, the hartal and now the crackdown and curfew and cross-firings . . . going mad! Tell me what's the point of this television at home when there's no power! Tell me what's the meaning of placing this radio set when there's no electricity! Tell me what's the point of opening this school bag when the school is closed for weeks or months! Tell me what's the point of sitting alive when all's going haywire. Everything lies occupied—all our lanes, school buildings, and our orchards and dargahs, even our graveyards. Last week Gulzar told me to shut up when I told him that I counted ten freshly dug graves in that qabristan near the shops! He'd kept shrieking that he hates to see the dead bodies and qabrs . . . shrieking so very hysterically at me as though I dug those graves!

6 p.m.

There goes the sun and there start off my mother's depressing talks. Last night I could hear her sobs and father telling her that all will be okay with our lives. Can't blame her; she fears for our lives. Weren't nani and nanu (grandmother and grandfather; in our village all my cousins call the two, nainn and budebub, but in our home Gulzar started calling them nani and nanu and I simply followed him!), telling us of Parveena's children picked up and then never got back! Gone is gone . . . they kept sighing! Will write again as they are sitting not too far and they going on looking at me in that worried way, as though peeping right into my head!

6.30 p.m.

Went to see if mother cooked anything. Nah, nothing cooked except that rice! She looking lost since morning. Even when father kept calling her 'Posh, Posh, Posh', she sat all too quiet. I really like my mother's name so much; like her name she's also like a lovely flower. Many times I call her Posh. Earlier she used to look angrily at me but not now. Says it's okay, so now even Gulzar has started calling her Posh and she doesn't react one bit.

7 p.m.

Till last week she was visiting the masjid for nimaz (namaz) and then sitting with those other women discussing crackdowns, reading the newspaper got along by Shiasta's mother, but now she sits all too glum. Can't stand that look on her face! Let me move out from here and peep out of the door towards the inner lane. Maybe Yaseena also is peeping out. Yes, yes, I can see her head with that blue-coloured hijab on, but she's been looking the other side. Can't say why but I do like her. She looks so simple, like a doll. Of course, I never played with dolls but seen them in those shops along the Boulevard and once saw so many dolls in the Polo View market but Yaseena looks like a real one . Don't know why she's always putting on that hijab, even in school. Maybe her mother forces her to . . . maybe screaming and shouting . . . these mothers can get so controlling! The way Yaseena keeps calling her mother Mummy . . . Mummy! I like her voice . . . really like her voice.

8 p.m.

Bijli (electricity) coming and going from evening but let me go on scribbling while it's there! Don't know what else to do or undo! Wondering why the MLA Meer janab lie to us that if these mohalla people elect him then he'll see to it that these lanes will be cleaned and bijli will come all hours . . . so much lies . . . nothing at all . . . garbage piles piling up and the stink around the lanes and the stray dogs barking, attacking, biting so many of us. That boy, Nazir, was telling me that Israelis also unleash dogs on Palestinians and so this *hukumat* doing the same here. Nazir knows much; after all, his father teaches in the Islamia College and my father just selling shawls and now nothing! Who buys shawls here and last time when he went selling them in Bangalore, he was beaten by the goondas there. Just can't forget that day when he came back in that bus with those two of our Kashmiri professors collecting money and then accompanying him all that way here.

10 p.m.

Maddening noise around! Crackdown! Gulzar wasn't moving away from the window . . . these security creatures started firing down the lane. Mother had been trying pulling him away but he not listening. When will father get back! Will write again. So many screaming, pellets hitting at doors and windows.

5 August 2016—9 a.m.

These last three days have been so maddening. My boi (brother) Gulzar still in hospital. Not sure whether he will ever see through that eye hit by pellets. Unmoving he kept sitting there, peeping out of the window, till mother shrieked but it was too late! Blood and more blood .And then his cries and shrieks and broken glass all over.

My brother, I love him too much but what could one do. I saw him being hit, but nothing I could do! Wrapped him in this shawl and rushed him out. All clinics' shutters down. Mother shrieked and shrieked, told that inspector janab blocking the way, that our Gulzar is dying, his eye bleeding and only then he let us rush him to that big hospital named after our long dead Maharaja Hari Singh . . . Gulzar been crying. Now no school for him. Now no homework for him. Now no more peeping out of the window!

Then grandmother had to take off, she went on crying: what's going to happen to Gulzar—how will he earn a living without eyesight! Doesn't she know I'll study hard and work as a bank clerk . . . keep counting money and look after Gulzar. Just want my school to open again. Can't wait. Want to start study and study and then start earning soon and very soon.

11 a.m.

No, I will never become a shawl weaver or seller! That's for sure. Want a proper job where I get a salary and so don't have to go about pleading. Hate the way father sitting worrying how to feed us and now of course Gulzar's one eye gone. Ruptured and ruined! Though that doctor they have got from Dilli kept telling us that he will do surgeries and then some 'roshni' will come back but I don't believe any of this. Gone is gone! As it is Gulzar was born so weak, my twin but half my height and all too bony. Now his eye gone. Can't look at the bandages across his face. Feel like kissing, hugging him, but the doctor janab told us that we should not put any pressure on his face.

Tell me what to do! Each time I sit with him on his hospital ward bed, I look around at the other children with damaged eyes my blood boils! My head starts throbbing with anger! I hate these dogs . . . these bloody dogs killing us. Why is this hukumat doing so much zulm! And yesterday as I sat holding Gulzar's hand, the television reporter came near us and like a mean woman kept asking Gulzar had he thrown stones at the security creatures! Poor Gulzar started stammering . . . my poor brother was simply sitting as always near the window with nothing at all in his hands. Not even a piece of tsot (bread) in his hands as rations had run out in our home! But that television woman with lipstick all over her ugly drooping lips couldn't understand what my brother was trying to say! Imagine that stupid fat woman even asked my brother how he felt getting hit in the eye! Is she mad! How would she feel if I boxed and punched her face! I wanted to shout at her but was too scared of the people around me. I could have been thrown into some jail or picked up and thrown into the missing lot. No, my brother and nor I, cannot ever be part of the stone- pelters. You know all that father wants is that we study and study and study. He keeps telling us that the very first word in the Quran is—Iqra—to read. One of his sister's son went with his poph (paternal aunt), all the way to Iran to study there but they are with money. We are not!

13 August—8 a.m.

Can't move out. Curfew all around, till the Nowhatta Chowk. Even last year, just before 15 August, no movement at all. Even birds dare not fly in the skies! How to go to the hospital and be with my brother. I'm really missing him. Know that grandparents have come down from our village in Ganderbal to be here with us but they are driving me mad with all sorts of silly questions. Throwing all their worries on my head! Just want to run from this room to the hospital and sit there with boi! But sitting here, listening to their rant! It's better if they had taken me back to our village. At least I would have been fishing in the Sindh River, and then cooking the catch. Yes, I remember every single detail when we were last there three years back . . . the shawl-weaving room and also the embroiderers and that argument that took off on the designing. Father hated the new complicated designs but those embroiderers told him that complicated weaves are much in demand in the markets of Dilli and Bambai. The way he looked at them and lashed out—yes, very complicated designs for those very complicated people! Then suddenly they all laughed in that simple carefree way! You know we Kashmiri have our own ways to find ways to laugh!

Why is grandmother been asking me what to cook. She knows there's only rice and some hokh syun (dried vegetables). Maybe in that side box on the shelf. Not sure of anything now. Can't keep answering all her questions. She's talking like a child, repeating that we all move to the village. Not even bothering to hear that if we leave this home, it will be gone forever. These security creatures will occupy it like they have occupied all the orchards and gardens! Nadeem's chai café is also occupied by them; now

they are sitting on all those chairs, ordering about. But she doesn't know
all this! And if I say anything more she starts chanting Sabr, sabr . . . yesterday she had started off reciting Lalla Arifa's verse on sabr. Have heard
it before a hundred times. And when I told her that those sabr-laden
lines would make some sense to me when I sit old like her she looked all
very upset, angrily reciting once again (for the hundredth time!) these
Lalla's lines.

> 'Patience, my son! is like a golden bowl;/Being costly, none doth dare
> purchase it./Patience, my son, is a mixture of salt, pepper and zira
> (spice);/It is bitter to taste, so who will taste it?'

She doesn't know that father has been reading Lalla's verse to us . . . one
verse after another. Don't know why he took to shawl selling. He knows so
much of poets and poetry. He should have been running some printing
press, bringing out akhbars. But he says that poets also die of sheer pov-
erty. Poetry very much like shawls doesn't sell!

14 August—10 a.m.
Sitting . . . sabr, awaiting some news to come from the hospital. How?
The mobile has been shut and the roads all sealed. Always these days,
before and after 15 August! What independence! Don't feel azaad at all
. . . not one bit! Don't know how many more days when Gulzar could
get discharged. Several days because they say that eye surgeries take
very long to heal and then when back here how will he manage. Maybe
grandparents take him with them to the village but then how will we
live without him. Impossible . . . already missing him. Wait till I become
a clerk and then look after him. Just let me study properly. Right now
I have to keep hearing my grandfather's constant reminders of a this or
that. Grandfather has been grumbling since early morning. Seems like
he is in competition with her . . . keeps looking out of the door and then
upwards at the sky, mumbling that ever since he is here from the village
no Jumma nimaz for him, no hearing of the sermon of the Mirwaiz because all roads leading to the Jami Masjid have been sealed. This, when
the Jami Masjid is so close but who can break curfews. He was muttering
that even eighty-year-olds are arrested and then made to rot in police
lockups.

25 August—11 a.m.

We got Gulzar back home last evening. But he looks so weak and bony. The doctors have removed the stained bandage, but he can't see through that eye. He is not even eating a thing though mother made some yakhni—I think she made it after months and I finished the entire bowl after Gulzar refused to eat. What has Gulzar been thinking? Why is he quivering seeing the broken window panes . . . why is mother not letting grandmother and grandfather see his damaged eye! Maybe they can't see that sight of that deadened eye. But weren't they telling me that they no longer scared of deaths and the dead, not even of graves and graveyards.

Gulzar is not letting mother move; she not leaving his side. One change is there, he's no longer calling her mouji, mouji . . ., but mummy because that other child lying on the next bed was calling his mother mummy and his father something else . . . yes, mummy and daddy! Heard many other Kashmiri children in the hospital calling their mother mummyji! Grandmother is saying that all our Kashmiri language is going because of so many outsiders stationed here, on our heads. She is telling me that these security fellows talk in some different language, nothing like us. Nah, nah, not Urdu, she understands a little bit of Urdu but she says it's some other language. Maybe Punjabi or Bihari. Anyway, not our headache for we don't have to speak to them. Just hear them shout and scream and yell at us as though we are their slaves and they our big masters! I must say I simply love my Kashmiri language. No match for it! But here in this diary I'm purposely using very little of our Kashmiri words because I'm writing this diary in English, so why mix and match. Father has been anyway telling us to respect and love all languages in the world, for then one can be called learned!

26 August—1 a.m.

I can't believe what I have been hearing right after Isha nimaz/night prayers . . . what four of them are discussing about me—that I should be sent off to Dilli so that I stay alive and safe! Can't believe what I have been hearing! Imagine thinking of shifting me from here. Where's the money! Last year we couldn't even go to Charar-i-Sharief for the Urs of Baba Nund Rishi, our Shaikh Nuruddin, our patron saint of the Valley, because there was no money for the tempo and Gulzar throws up in the bus. So how will they take me to Dilli! For what! Hide me where and for what! Where will I study . . . how will I ever become a bank clerk! Let me ask them directly what they want! Now can't sleep the whole night . . . let morning arrive then I'll scream. Howow can they throw me out, out of my own place? If they want to get rid of me, then I rather run to Ganderbal . . . our village . . . our people. And from there I take a bus to Gulrez where maas (maternal aunt) lives. Imagine making plans of shifting me from here to there without even taking the trouble of asking me!

How I wanted to go to Charar ever since father had been reading out to us our Shaikh Nuruddin verses. Why don't I shift there. With me I could take books and read aloud to the all about his mystic ways. Why not! If they can make plans to shift me to Dilli, I can make my plans to shift to Charar and sit there! Wait . . . wait, I have all the stuff on him . . . let me jot it all down here . . . right here from these two volumes by our history writer GMD Sufi. Here I go . . . so much on him with me. These lines of his—'By bowing down, thou shalt not become a Rishi; / The pounder in the rice mill did not ever raise up its head'.

Also the way Shaikh Nuruddin hits out at hypocrisy. You know, when he was invited for a feast, he reached there much before the appointed time and in ragged clothes. The servants not recognizing him, would not permit him to enter, and he had to go back to take his food at home. When all had sat for the sumptuous dinner, Shaikh Nuruddin was specially sent for. He came, this time, in a flowing 'chugha' (cloak) and was given the seat of honour. But instead of eating the food, he stretched forth his sleeves and put them on the plates. The people were astonished at the sight and asked him the reason. He'd said 'The feast was not really for Nuruddin but for the long sleeves!'

You know these books carrying so much of about us, about our beautiful place . . . if they dare to shift me from my home I will carry away these two books but how, they are so heavy. And mother will see . . . she will know! Mother doesn't miss a single detail, her eyes go all over. O my Allah, o my Rasool help me!

26 August—3 a.m.
Can't sleep. My eyes not closing at all! Been drinking water but feeling so angry. Strange people in my useless family. Till last evening they wouldn't even let me step out till the Nowhatta Chowk, fearing I'll be killed by these security creatures like they had shot dead Tufail Matto in 2010, or I'll get

picked up for interrogation like other boys, but now they want to send me to India! What is wrong with them! Though poph has been calling us to their home in Pampore, we not sent, not even when she was leaving for Haj. What has got wrong with their heads! They are talking of my great future if I live away from my Srinagar! What's got wrong with them!

26 August—6 a.m.
Not slept at all . . . can't . . . the eyes not closing . . . restless, anger growing. But why aren't these four up and starting off with their nimaz . . . look at the way mouj is somewhat turning, clasping her head. Why is no one up and about!

26 August—7 a.m.
There gets up father and sits hunched. Let him walk out of the room and I'll just start off writing. He is always asking me why I am writing so much when schools are shut. Old man doesn't understand if I didn't unleash all this anger in my diary, my head would have burst! Last evening when I broke open the last walnut with me, I kept looking at it as though my brain got stuffed in there. Have you closely watched a walnut from inside? Do that, and see how the brain is made and how it can break into pieces if hit. Let me hold my head tight. No, I don't want it to burst open!

Why am I crying! I cannot cry like this. I am already so tall and I got to take care of my brother if not of these old people, even if they have those devilish plans of shunting me out of here! I think they are going all too old and tense.

29 August—7 p.m.
Couldn't write last two or three days. These days, mother been looking at me, weeping in that ongoing way. Grandparents been reading the Quran all day. I sat and argued with father for hours, but he looked so upset and sad that I couldn't argue any further. He kept repeating I will be able to live much better there, in some school type place near some Taj building in Dilli. Nah, nah, he kept muttering that it isn't the Taj Mahal but some other building for boys education. Several Kashmiri shawl sellers go there for Jumma nimaz and that's how he'd heard of it. They teach the Quran and also English and many other subjects and give free food and free stay.

30 August—6 a.m.
Nothing to say or write. Nothing very much to keep or leave behind . . .
certain I will not be able to come back here for months. Why they are
telling me all stupid silly lies—that they'll come down to Dilli once it gets
too cold here. Do they have money? Do they know that all these shawls
are lying unsold wouldn't be sold so very easily—what in this ongoing
curfew.

30 August—1 p.m.
Want to go one last time towards Badam Wari with Gulzar but I know we
won't be allowed to, his eye injury is still not okay. The wound still all too
raw, and he's lost confidence to even walk about this room so to walk out
would get difficult for him to cope with, even if the curfew is lifted for a
couple of hours.

31 August—9 p.m.
The curfew was lifted till afternoon. And mother muttered rather too
nervously that we should go to the Nishat gardens, carrying rice and
haaq she'd been cooking. No, said father, and then quite out of the blue,
suggested our going to Kasb-i-Mah. After all, we have never been there
before although it stands close to the Chashme Shahi springs. Before
their arguments could go any further, cries from outside that curfew re-
imposed. Now we can't get out. Father took off telling us in his usual patient way, distracting us with details to Kasb-i-Mah—that it was built by
Mughal Prince Dara Shikoh after he was greatly influenced by his sufi
teacher who had come from some far off place called Badakhshan. He
never went back. Stayed on here till his death. Even I want to stay on in
my Kashmir till my death.

The more details I heard to the place, I just wanted to go see it.
I kept shrieking and shrieking. Don't know what happened to me that
time, more so as grandfather said that I should visit it in my dreams!
Grandmother added that I join the police and then get stationed there
and then see it properly! Don't know whether it was a taunt! Of course,
it was a taunt. A bloody slap on my face but determined that I was to be
taken there! You know this old couple getting bitter, taking out it on me.
Obviously they can't say a thing to injured, ailing Gulzar.

I told mother that I will go to Dilli only after they take me there. There was absolute silence in the room, I don't know for how many minutes. Then she surprised us by coming up with a getaway plan—saying that only she and grandmother would go with me as then it will be much easier to go from the lanes, and if the cops do ask about curfew-breaking, she can tell them that she's taking her old mother and young son to the hospital. More than that she hinted that as two women—one old and the other not-too-young it would far less easier for them to accompany me than if I was being accompanied by two men—my father and grandfather.

Risky, risky, is all I could hear from grandparents sitting at one end, on the jane-maaz/prayer mat. Mother couldn't help countering all those warnings by saying that utmost we'll be shot dead on way! Saying this, she hugged Gulzar and then tied the hijab on her head and covered her chest with a chaddar and then almost simultaneously threw another chaddar on grandmother. Don't ask me why those big chaddars on their frail chest, with their breasts dangling low. That too on a hot humid day. But then couldn't dare ask any queries as the entire home atmosphere was getting tense. Not letting any of the forewarnings and warnings come in way, we set off. The lanes were deserted except for a few mad rebel creatures like us. Mother held my hand very tight as though the cops would snatch me from her. Grandmother walked somewhat slowly, holding the chaddar tight . . . very tightly. Only her small eyes could be seen.

Though the CRPF van driving past us slowed down when they spotted us but didn't yell, halt or shoot orders. Then very suddenly one of the jawans rushed towards us from the roadside bunker. Mother furthered her hold on me, and muttered that we continue walking and not stopping. Not even when he asked in broken Hindustani where we off to in this curfew! She looked back and pointed towards grandmother . . . throwing her old prescription papers at him. He looked at us again, and then towards grandmother limping by now. And as he walked back briskly to the bunker, we walked ahead, but all too tense.

I can't describe what a long, tense walk. To the Dal Gate. Then further towards the Dal Lake and then further on that road ahead. Where curfew seemed lifted as the bazaar was opening, several shops' shutters opening up. We hired a big auto till the end of the Boulevard and then again we had to walk. On those roads auto rickshaws were not allowed. Only big cars driving past us. Also many military jeeps. Somewhat scary. All those walking on the road looked very tense and could see many walking with a hunch.

At home, mother and grandmother would utter-mutter constantly, so many arguments between the two, but not that noon. Strange quiet even as the walk turned tougher; what, with us having to cover another stretch. Check posts in between, where we were frisked. Imagine frisked in such harsh humiliating ways in our own country by outsiders.

Then that building out there—Kasb-i-Mah. What a beautiful structure had stood out all too suddenly. There's the Dal Lake down below and the range of mountains standing tall and lofty and somewhere in between this structure.

Several foreign women were getting off from a big car, wearing very little on their bodies. Why were mother and grandmother going on and on staring at their legs!

It got too embarrassing for me. Walked away from them, I stood close to these foreigners, hearing the guide tell them all those details of this place which father had already told us. Let me try and repeat what he was telling them—'This school of sufism, was said to be the only one of its kind in the whole of Asia and Central Asia. Dara Shikoh had built this unique school of sufism - called the "Kasb i -Mah". Nowadays it is also called the Pari Mahal! This Mughal Prince built it at the instance of his spiritual teacher, Akhund Mulla Mohammad Shah, who came from Badakhshan'. Then that guide went on talking more and more. This time details to the sufis, as those women rolled their eyes, hearing all those details.

'Our Mughal Emperor Jehangir focused on the very simplicity that these sufis not just believed in, but actually practiced in everyday life. This emperor wrote this about our sufis, in his memoirs - "though they have not religious knowledge or learning of any sort yet they possess simplicity and are without pretence. They abuse no one. They restrain the tongue of desire and foot of seeking. They eat no flesh, they have no wives and always plant fruit bearing trees in the fields so that men may benefit by them, themselves desiring no advantage." ' This guide continued showing off his knowledge as those women kept taking his pictures with the great looking mobile phones in their hands . . . 'Abu'l Fazl has also written extensively about his meeting with Wahid sufi, "Here an enlightened anchorite has come to my view—for thirty years he has, in an unnoticed corner, been gathering happiness on an old mat." ' And then he came up with another big name. Our very big history man, GMD Sufi, has written these very important lines about our sufis —'deeply imbued with sufism of the age and country from which they emigrated these Sayyids and their followers seem to have stimulated the tendency to mysticism for which Vedantism and Buddhism had already paved the way'.

I could easily become a guide. Been thinking of this guide idea all the way when we walked back. Also, why doesn't my father become a guide. He knows all these things about our sufis and poets and about our so many places. I will try and tell him all this. You know I saw these women giving the guide lots of rupees which he kept stuffing in his two pockets. But he didn't look rich. His shoes were all torn, yet he walked around as though he some hero. But yes, his hair very well cut. Stylish. Like Shahrukh Khan's . . . When those foreign women got busy taking pictures of flowers and trees growing around, I told this guide that he looks a little like Shahrukh Khan. I thought he would be happy but all he did was to mutter, 'Can't stand him after I saw his one photo where's drinking that bad stuff . . . and in another photo he's kissing some doggy!'

31 August—11.30 p.m.

Got very tired writing so much. Also to say that ever since we have got back, nobody is speaking at home. Maybe they are tense or very exhausted. Even when I told father that he should become a guide and then there'll be no problem in our lives, he didn't even look at me. Nor did he ask me a word about my trip to Kasb-i-Mah. All that he said that we'll be leaving for Dilli very soon. Dont know whether in a day or two days.

I wanted to talk to him, but he lay down. Yes, I know he's been pretending to sleep. Though even now I can see him holding his head and tossing and turning.

2

Reaching New Delhi

4 September 2016—2 p.m.

Haven't touched you, my diary, for the last so many days. How could I!
Couldn't write one word, though been so terribly restless to write . . . to
go on writing, throw out all possible thoughts. Now stopping in Jammu
for the day, sitting in a shop near the bus stand, and while father is saying
his nimaz, I am writing. It is owned by one of our distant relatives from
our village, so safe . . . they have been discussing how Kashmiris from
Srinagar can be killed here by goondas all around. Yes, yes, they told me
I'm looking all very Kashmiri! But I'm a Kashmiri, so have to look one!
One of the shawl sellers here told us that he doesn't take his sons out of
Kashmir because of the attack fears. Yes, yes, he looked very nervous
and went on saying that if we look like Kashmiris we get attacked! And
if we don't look like Kashmiris, then also we will be attacked and called
Rohingya refugees! This is madness! Don't know what type of refugee
I'll be called—whether I'll be called a Kashmiri or a Rohingya in that big
city, Dilli!

Already missing my Kashmir, my people. Missing my brother, the
most. You know when I was leaving home, mother cried and though
Gulzar also burst out but doctors had warned us that there shouldn't be
any pressure on the stitches. You know his stitches still are not healed, pus
is coming out from the upper eye lid. When my bag was all stuffed with
clothes, with two small packets of walnuts, and also with three of the poetry books that father gave from his book shelf, we had to quietly go out
in the afternoon as the curfew would be re-imposed. The bus to Dilli was
leaving at dawn, so we walked till Lal Chowk and from there we took the
tempo to Hazratbal and spent the night on the steps of the shrine, though
for many minutes father kept walking along on the lawns, by the side of
the shrine.

The Diary of Gull Mohammad. Humra Quraishi, Oxford University Press. © Oxford University Press India 2023.
DOI: 10.1093/oso/9789391050269.003.0003

You know my youngest poph, Saleema Jan, lives close to the Kashmir University compound in the Naseem Bagh locality, but father said it doesn't look okay if we go there knocking un-announced. Mobiles are useless for us, still not working. All mobile connectivity dead. He said why to disturb them in the midst of so much chaos. It's better we sit at the Hazratbal lawns and pray till dawn and then reach the bus stand. Mother had packed rice and some haaq leftovers from our dinner in a plastic bag, and we sat on the lawns . . . couldn't eat much. So many stray dogs all around. We kept hearing what those others sitting around been telling us, that the hukumat doing all this, like Israelis are doing to Palestinian refugees—leaving stray dogs in their midst to bite and bark and make living impossible.

And when I looked around all too upset, as always, my father stopped eating and started off in his usual way of trying to distract me, telling me why our Hazratbal shrine is so very important for us. Yes, when we were walking there I could see many people praying and also crying loudly. Many mothers were muttering prayers for the safety of their children. My mother must be praying for me at home. At least she has my brother with her. But I'll have no one with me. I will be left all alone.

Yes, yes, Allah will be with me! My Prophet Rasool too! I really and really wanted to see my Rasool's hair in Hazratbal, but we were told it can be seen only on some fixed day. And even before I could ask father any further details, he was himself telling me how our Prophet Rasool's sacred hair got here, how the moi-e-muqaddus was brought to the Valley. And he kept telling me I should tell all those details (to how our Rasool's hair reached Kashmir) to my class fellows in Dilli. He's sure nobody would have all those details—happened many years back. And father kept muttering that today nobody talks about these things of the past . . . you know it came here because of one person, Syed Abdullah, who had left Medina a long time ago around 1635, and then settled in some place called Bijapur, near Hyderabad. And when Syed Abdullah died, his son Syed Hamid inherited the relic. He kept it with him but not for long. Because of the Mughal kings' invasions in the region he was left poor and without his properties, so he decided to sell it off to a Kashmiri businessman, Khwaja Nooruddin Eshai . . . he is also called Khwaja Nooruddin Ashwari. But before this Kashmiri man could travel with it here, Mughal Badshah Aurangzeb got to know of the rare possession in the hands of that businessman and he spared no time in confiscating it from him and sending it off to be placed in the dargah of Khwaja Moinuddin Chishti situated in Ajmer. He also had Eshai janab imprisoned in Dilli. And then later one day the Badshah realized what he did was wrong and gave orders for his release, and for him to carry the relic to our Kashmir. But by then, Eshai janab had died in prison. The Badshah then tried to make up for his big mistake, by not just sending the relic to our Kashmir, but also that man's dead body to our Kashmir for burial. Eshai 's daughter Inayat Begum was made the caretaker–custodian of the relic and since then, it's her descendants who have been taking care of it.

Such a long story and will try remember all these details to tell those Dilli boys.

8 p.m.
Don't know who will take care of my boi. Hopeless type of sorrow lies in my home. And when I said I'm feeling very nervous about this journey and what lies ahead, my father kept telling me that Dilli has many things.

Stopping here. Will write again as they are all staring at me. I don't want them to snatch my diary and read. I'll die if they read even a word! Now they calling me to sit with them. Will try and write in the bus but not too sure.

Can't tell you how crowded the bus was when we came from Srinagar. We were smelling of sweat and what not! Hadn't bathed for many days. Very little water was coming in our kitchen pipe and then mouj kept shrieking that I'll catch a cold or chill and can't fall ill because of this journey . . . her thinking getting all too strange! Even noticed that father been walking around with a big hunch. Nah, nah, he isn't every old. He doesn't tell his actual age, says all that's not important but I think he must be around 40 or less. Heard grandparents discuss that he was married off rather late according to our Kashmiri ways because those days there were too many killings taking place, and he was very depressed. He was going for depression treatment for months . . . even now he looks so sad. But my friend Bilal had told me that his father was married when he was only 20 and his father also walked with a big hunch. Oh! no, have been noticing so many of us are walking with a hunch. I have got to be careful. I have to be strong, have to take care of my brother. That's why agreed for this going to Dilli. Maybe I get a job there after I study very, very hard and then he wouldn't have to work. My brother left with only one eye! Don't know why this happened to him. You know my brother loves our Allah, our Rasool. I feel lazy going on saying nimaz but not he! When in no-curfew time he loves walking to the Jami masjid but was now, of course, saying all his nimaz at home . . . will write again because father is looking upset with me, they are already starting with the rice and shorba or whatever else is there. I think goshtaba too . . . haven't eaten it for years. Yes, yes, I think last time at the wazwan hosted by my aunt Saleema Jan's family for their daughter Insha's nikah . . . will leave for the bus stop as soon as we over with the dinner—bus to Dilli starts at 11 p.m.

7 September—7 p.m.

What a terrible journey and can't describe what a terrible place I have landed in! Too much to say. Right now, running to the 'latrine' as they call it here in this stupid, cramped madrasa. Latrine is already occupied. They been saying, that young boy got here only a few hours before us but been in there shitting for one hour!

Imagine their stupidity! For so many boys there is only one latrine and only one 'ghusalkhana' (washroom or bathroom)! Have to control, but for how long. Let me try distracting myself by writing some more. Father had to leave soon; as soon as the maulvis told him in those half whispers that they would get into trouble because of a bearded Kashmiri man in their madrasa for too long . . . problems and questioning could start off and land them in big trouble and the madrasa could also be closed down as a lot of the sarkari mantris or santris live very close by. My poor father kept kissing my head and maybe he was crying for I felt my hair was wet. He kept telling them that he wants to discuss my studies with them but they kept muttering that 4 September had just passed by and so many cops are around in the area. We couldn't see any cop but were told that they come there in 'plain clothes'! Don't know what they meant! You know when he pleaded with them once again they said that after 4 September bombings in America, all Muslims are under watch! Yes, yes, those bombings took place many years ago but Muslims are still hounded all over the world. Hunched, he walked away after holding me tight for many minutes and then before going, he gave these maulvis here those two walnut packets. Why did he have to give our walnuts to these two maulvis! Can't stand their very look! They almost shooed him away but then at least he didn't have to eat the watery daal and fat rotis that I had to somehow eat. Have to run to the latrine before it all comes out here on the mat!

7 September—9 p.m.
Not well. Not one bit. Told these maulvis that no more of their daal and rotis for me. You should have seen how they looked at me!
Their words so very harsh—Imagine, praying five times a day but said some terribly hurtful things to me—they even refused to make boiled rice or phirni with the leftover rice and that watery milk stored in that old ice box they sit guarding all day. Can't write, nor can I say my nimaz. My stomach is paining so much. I know they'll force me for nimaz but can't stand. You know here they don't even say nimaz but namaz. What a place! I want to throw off this kurta on me. Too thick and can see some rash sort of thing all over my neck and chest, but can't sit here without a kurta. Yes, all boys wearing long kurtas and pyjamas and even topis! Why this madness . . . so hot here! Want to throw away all my clothes and run towards some river. In the evening, I'd asked one of the boys if they have some lake or river nearby, but he gave me one of those looks as though I was talking some nonsense. Said river Yamuna flows not too far away but very, very dirty!

8 September—8 a.m.: I lay on the floor with these boys all night . . . couldn't sleep. Don't know how many times had to rush to the latrine . . . now no water in the latrine! Don't know what to do! I want to get back to my Srinagar. Told the younger of the two maulvis—Bakhtawar mia—to dial my father's mobile, but he said there's no balance in his phone. At least that older maulvi, Shafi sahib behaved more helpful, tried my father's number but kept saying the bell not passing. Maybe my father hasn't left Dilli and maybe he comes again to meet me before he goes back. I will go back with him. What's here for me—no food, no school, no friends, and no proper books. Nothing at all! Here, the boys go on and on chanting the verses I know by heart. They know nothing about my Kashmir. They know nothing! No radio, no television, can't even play outside! No, no curfew around as I am seeing cars and lots of people walking up and down on the big road. What do I do here! It's better to die a hundred times in my Srinagar, then it be alive here! Silly joke on . . . no school . . . just fooling the children. Though one of the older boys told me that till two years back they had two full time teachers for teaching English, Mathematics, and

Hindi, but now no money for teachers. Maybe they catch hold of some part time teacher for English. Let's see what English he teaches.

9 September—2 p.m.

Stomach is a little better after they finally listened to me. Cooked khichri for everyone. What a relief. But only and only khichri. No curd. No buttermilk. Nah, nothing else. And one of the nimazis who works in some nearby shop told the maulvis that for all stomach problem they should make us have *Anaars* and Bel-sherbets! The maulvis looked amused—first time in all these days I saw them smiling—after that man told them that lots of Bel (Stone Apple) trees and *Anaar* (Pomegranate) shrubs are growing nearby, in the compound of that some big minister sahib. Maulvi sahibs chuckling—'Why will that mantri sahib donate fruits to us! No, no election time. We are Muslims and these people hate us . . . will get some *ilzamaats* flung at us! Better to have our own galla paani!'

10 September—3 p.m.

No, father didn't come back after dropping me here that evening. Maybe he is already travelling back home; after all, he'd come all the way only to drop me here. Who will buy shawls here in the monsoons! Maybe he too isn't well . . . sitting in sorrow like I am. Maybe he's staying in the Nizamuddin basti and visits me after a day or two. Maybe not, because he's also scared of the people here; after all, he's been hearing how the Kashmiris are getting hounded. Yes, he looks Kashmiri from a distance. Missing him so much.

10 September—11 p.m.

Somehow I gained confidence to ask the old maulvi sahib if I could myself dial father's mobile number, from his phone. At first the maulvi looked at me sternly but then all too suddenly nodded. I dialled my father's mobile number, but the bell wouldn't pass. Then he also dialled and re-dialled the number. And sat shaking his head. Quite obviously he couldn't get through. And what surprised me is that he asked if I'd have any other number with me—of my mother or brother or of my grandfather. No, only mother had a mobile, but she sold it off many months back and nobody else has a mobile in the family. The maulvi looked at me with some sort of sympathy and then asked if I wanted to go with the two older boys of the madrasa, Shamshad and Shakeel, to the nearby market—the Khan Market! I jumped with joy but then had to put on that horrible synthetic topi on my head and also change into a long kurta. Don't ask me why the maulvis saw to it that all the boys wear below-the- knees long kurtas. '*Shareef lago . . . baihuda battameez nahin!*' (look decent and not like indecent loafers) was maulvi Shafi's pet one-liner. The boys took care of me while we crossed the main crossing and then walked along the side walk. I kept looking around . . . couldn't control staring at the clothes those girls and women were wearing. No, nobody in hijabs or wrapped in chaddars but looking very much like those foreign women I saw at Kasb-i -Mah. Even the men in pants and jeans and walking about all too confidently. Two men stopped us and then sneered, calling us, 'madrasa wallahs!' One of them pointed his hand towards my skull cap and shrieked 'Kharku!' I wanted to shriek back, but Shamshad and Shakeel pulled me one side and started telling me that I have got to get used to hearing all this rubbish. Shamshad even showed his injured wrist and said that he was hit in the park by some goons, when he refused to chant Jai Shri Ram!

We sat down on the pavement and then bought one orange bar from the money we were carrying to buy 250 gm of mutton from a shop in Khan market. It was fun to take turns licking the drops melting away. But then the fun disappeared when those scooter men came again and stood near us. This time calling us 'You Musalmaan pillas . . . out of here. You creatures in our Khan Market area! Only for VVIPs and not for you all Musalmaans. Out or will break your bones! Will fling you right into your Pakistan!'

Just then some big person's big car was passing. It halted. And many police wallahs jumped out from a jeep and took control of the situation. Threw those men in their jeep and asked us to immediately return to our madrasa. We ran back, without the meat!

And I just sat back and couldn't control the flow of tears. Wanted to go back home. To my Kashmir!

The maulvi sahibs were very curious to know who could have helped madrasa children in this mahaul. They kept on muttering names of two 'Musalmaan' big persons in the sarkar but then quickly added that they don't ever come here to this madrasa for the Jumma nimaz so why would they help out the madrasa children!

This hadsaa (incident) was discussed by the maulvis with whoever came here for the maghrib nimaz/evening nimaz. I can't tell you how much it was discussed. After all, they were desperately keen to know that who could have helped the madrasa children. Finally, their curiosity somewhat settled when one of the retired thanedars, who now worked as a security guard in the nearby big hotel came for his nimaz, and said— 'Know who could this savior be. No, he is not a Muslim but a Sardar Singh sahib who is very good to us Musalmaans. He has got security from the sarkar because he is a big known writer so his life in big danger. Always he goes about with a jeep full of police wallahs. He must be the one. Yes, for sure. And he lives very near the Khan Market and there every other evening'.

Suddenly the two maulvis raised their hands in prayer mode, as though praying for the Sardar sahib's well-being! Kept chanting—Shukar Allah!

12 September—7 p.m.
I didn't want to write anything for the last couple of days. What to write except that after days meat was cooked here. One motor mechanic sahib, whom these boys call Khan sahib, had got along mutton qeema all too well wrapped in newspapers. Can't say much about the qeema because anyway I don't like the sight of raw meat, but poor man was going on and on telling the maulvis that it wasn't minced beef but pure mutton! What was the need for him to go on assuring and re-assuring them in this silly way. He was sweating as he was taking off those layers and layers of paper near-stuck around the qeema. Telling the maulvis that though it is mutton, but he could have been lynched if one of the men on the bus had cried out beef! After hearing him with all those details I didn't want to touch that qeema dish and had only some rice and Pudina-chutney which I only made after plucking off Pudina-pattees (Mint leaves) growing along the courtyard and then crushing then on the sill–batta in the kitchen. My hands were smelling of those leaves. Good fresh smell.

13 September—9 a.m.
So much of noise early morning. Again that poor little boy from Firozabad, Abuzair, was getting scolded after he cried out that he can't read as he can't see properly. He looks so sad and so very tiny, and these boys telling me that he was making bangles in some bangle factory there,

but then when his mother died his father left him here forever. They were saying he was coughing very badly and falling ill with high fever. Abuzair can't read properly and even that other boy, Zulfikhar, saying he needs a 'chashma'(spectacles) but maulvi sahib scolding them so much and repeatedly screaming that where's the money for chashmas and eye doctors! He went on and on saying this is a madrasa and not a hospital . . . no money with us!

But strangely in the midst of all this, last evening heard maulvi sahib telling the nimazis that he's collecting money to paint this madrasa all green! Saw three or four of them even giving many rupees to him for painting this little madrasa in Islamic colours! Saw maulvi's face looking all very radiant and then he spoke only and only of Jannat (heaven), and how these men who'd donated will sure go upwards towards heaven!

13 September—5 p.m.

The entire afternoon, that old maulvi sahib had been scolding Abuzair for not wearing a topi and long kurta and also for not reading properly! Poor boy tried to say that his head is full of boils and that he has no other kurta and that he can't see properly. Maulvi sahib seemed to have got blood pressure, and before he could slap that child, I couldn't control my anger and stood up and shouted in that hysterical way like I did at home when mother would scold my brother.

Thankfully just then that motor mechanic, Khan sahib, arrived for his evening nimaz and probably understood the happenings and made maulvi sip lots of water and told him that he'll take all the boys for eye check-up. Maulvi sahib's eyes almost popped out before he muttered, 'Where's money with us . . . just collected fifteen hundred because this place needs a fresh coat of paint but see so much of confusion and chaos!'

Settling the glass brimming with water, next to the maulvi's lips, Khan sahib pointed to Abuzair's boils and also to his watery eyes, 'Maulvi sahib, why waste on paints . . . why green or any other colour . . . this poor child looking so frail and ill.' Then, he went on to say that he will be taking all of us to some big doctor sahib who is an eye doctor. 'Free and totally free . . . bilkul muft!' He kept saying, 'I settle all his car problems, even taught driving to his begum sahiba. He in charge of that big government hospital. He's travelling to Vilayat for a conference but will be back in about ten days and I'll take all these children there. He's a good man.' The maulvi

again muttered, 'Is he a Sunni or Shia sahib?' This time that motor mechanic withdrew that glass from the maulvi's mouth before saying— 'No,
he's neither Sunni nor Shia. He's a Hindu . . . a very good Hindu doctor
sahib.'

14 September—4 p.m.
From morning such big talks that some master is coming to teach us
English. He came so late . . . said he coming during lunch-hour from
some office he works in. He taught so very little. Nothing! Just went on
repeating ABCD . . . I learnt all this hundred years back. I would have
taught this master much more than what he was teaching us. Useless!
When I told this to the old maulvi sahib he told me that I shouldn't have
come here at all if I was so very far ahead! Don't know what he meant by
all this! Shakeel told us that earlier they had a very good English teacher,
but the madrasa management couldn't pay him the regular salary, so that
man left, and this new person would come for only one hour and only
once or twice a week, so obviously no great English teaching. Shakeel
also said that this maulvi sahib had gone with him to some big sarkari office for special grants for madrasa education but was shooed off from the
gates! Why? Because he is bearded and wearing a shervani and skull cap!

15 September—10 a.m.
What's happened to maulvi sahib . . . reading the Urdu newspaper aloud
and then looking at me in some strangely inquisitive way. Usually no
newspaper comes here to this madrasa; maybe this one left back by one of
the nimazis who carries newspapers and even sits under the shed reading
them. Today maulvi sahib called me and touched my head and patted my
back, saying—just been reading what tortures you Kashmiris are going
through. Zulm, zulm on you all!

16 September—8 a.m.
From yesterday, he's been somewhat kind to me but who wants charity!
You know over two years back when floods hit and those flood waters
had ruined my Srinagar, some Dilli minister had come to our Srinagar
and father had taken Gulzar and me to hear his speech where he kept on
talking of giving us relief packages! Nah! Nothing reached us! Not even
his words, because as father rightly said that empty words and useless

promises can't fill stomachs. I don't want anything from this maulvi except that he makes me talk to toth and sends me back to my home. Here useless for me. I can never become a bank person with these no studies! There's not even a black board or a school bag or copies or books!

16 September—9 p.m.

Some activity or as these people say some raunaq in the evenings as several office persons come here for their evening nimaz/asar nimaz, on their way back from office to home. At times, they sit in small groups and discuss what problems Muslims are facing and then all look very, very sad. Most of them say that there is no water supply and electricity in their mohallas. One of these men had carried lots of Jamuns for us. He said that he has two or three Jamun trees in his village home. He was telling others about some elections in his village and all Muslims have to vote against the Sanghis! He was repeatedly telling them that they should not get fooled by these Sanghis. He kept on calling them dushmans and big, big enemies of the Musalmaans!

11 p.m.

Forgot to write that the same lot were doing so much talk of one big leader—Pandit Nehru. You know they were saying that after this death all's gone haywire.

They saying that their mothers and fathers didn't even think of migrating to the new country, Pakistan, because they were sure that Pandit Nehru will take really good care of the Muslims of India, which he did. He was a very good man, who cared for the masses of the country.

Then, one of the nimazis kept talking how his khala (maternal aunt), fell ill while crossing the borders and how they managed to get back home in Purani Dilli. They didn't let her go, though she had to be married there. Her marriage had to be cancelled, and she didn't ever marry . . . died in his home only last Monday.

Others went on narrating how the Partition ruined so many Muslim families.

Adding that what the Partition couldn't do is being done today! They saying they have told their children not to talk of Pakistan in their schools and colleges otherwise any terror charge can be thrown on their heads!

Maulvi sahibs said that if only Mahatma Gandhi was alive today, then the Musalmaans would be so very carefree. '*Bahut acche insaan thei . . . bahut nayaab . . . bahut umda aadmi!*' (a very good person…a very great, precious, good person.)

17 September—8 p.m.
For the first time, a woman entered this madrasa. Of course, lots of women walking on the main road and many walking towards the hotel gates. All wear skirts or those tight, tight jeans. Once the maulvi sahib saw me staring at them while I was sweeping the pavement outside and he gave a long lecture. Imagine telling me that I should keep control on my eyes!

He doesn't say a word to that old hunched man who comes on Jumma nimaz day and after his nimaz keeps sitting near the shed and staring at us boys. Somehow the way he stares doesn't make one feel okay. When I said this to Shakeel, he also nodded but said that man called Mansoor Mia is a chacha of one of the management persons so can't complain against him. He also added that I should be careful, that man doesn't peep into the ghusalkhana! 'If he does, then kick him there!' When I asked where, he told me to keep shut!

Okay, let me write about this woman. She looked very poor and wanted to work here, cook and clean and wash utensils—but maulvis kept shaking their heads, saying that no woman should be seen in the madrasa. Then, she said that she wanted to leave her two sons here but maulvis again saying no. This time saying that there are too many children and too little rations. She left without saying anything but looked very sad.

18 September—4 p.m.
Suddenly lots of activity since dawn, right after the fajr nimaz time. Maulvis gave brooms to the three older boys and they started off; transferring dust, from the veranda to the courtyard and then towards the gate. Another two boys sprinkling water all along the veranda floor and then mopping. Though the bare floors are kept pretty okay, this was the first time that I could see so much of the cleaning. Why this sudden cleaning? Was told that some sarkari person was coming here for some inspection. Maulvis looked excited but also very tense. Sent off Shamshad and Shakeel to the corner chai shop to get biscuits. They asked me if I wanted to go along with them, but I didn't want to because everybody on the road stares at us and some even point to our topis. I just don't like it. In my

Srinagar we putting on topis but nobody dares stare in this way; but see how they look at us as though we are some strange creatures. I feel very uneasy and upset by their glares.

18 September—10 p.m.
That government person came only in the evening. He asked the maulvis all our names and the books we read. Before leaving he ate all the biscuits and gulped down many cups of chai. Also told these maulvis that next day there was some competition in the sarkari school on the other side of some big garden. I think they called it Lodi garden and if they want they could send three or four boys for it. Some education minister will come and give prizes too.

19 September—7 p.m.
So many mosquitoes here! They'd been discussing how last year one of the boys had died of some new disease, some bimari called dengue! Before I could think any further of dengue and deaths, one of the boys made a pulp of Neem leaves and told us that we should rub that paste on our bodies, but as I was midway putting that paste, maulvis announced they keen to go for the government school function so that they could request the minister for some new books or teaching grants for the madrasa. They looked around at us and decided to take along four or five children. I also raised my hand and added that I would take part in the writing competition as in my Srinagar school I was always standing first.

They nodded. We went along. I could walk with difficulty, as the chappals were hurting. On the way we stopped at a book store in Khan Market and I must say that shopkeeper was very good to us. I wanted a big copy to write in, for that competition and so did Shakeel and Shamshad, and Ishtiaq but we only had thirty rupees. Ten rupees less. Maulvi sahib gave us only that much, and that too after counting and re-counting the notes a hundred times.

The shopkeeper smiled and let us take all the copies and said we would pay him later. Nah, nah, he wasn't a Muslim. I read the shop's name on that big board—Nirulas or something like that. These boys say that he's some Punjabi, but I must say that after days I met such a polite and simple man.

We reached that government school, after crossing the big gardens made by some Lodi Badshah. And there, other children were wearing school uniforms Only four of us were dressed in kurta pyjamas and topis on our heads. We were immediately called the madrasa children and then all the other children kept away from us, even sat away from us. I didn't like the way the main person there—principal of that big government school—looked at me in that horrible insulting way when they told him that I was a Kashmiri child.

I hated this man. How can he look after schools when he hates children. After we were given two samosas each and a small bottle of water, we were told to write an essay in Hindi or English on some place which we would like or want others to visit. Shakeel, Shamshad, and Ishtiaq said that they wouldn't be able to write on anything other than their village and that too in Urdu. And even before the organizers could look towards me, I had decided to write on the sufi dargahs of my Kashmir... Will write again all those remaining details, time for nimaz. And though I am praying so many times a day but Allah mia is not listening to me! Don't know when on earth He will find time to listen to me and send me back to my Kashmir!

19 September—10 p.m.
What's going wrong with people in this Dilli! I wrote about sufi dargahs, but the way they looked at me in that strange way, saying that sufi babas are now all dead and gone. They told me that it's best to write about smart cities! But I told them that I want to write about our sufi dargahs. I told them I know so much about them. So wrote all I knew but you should have seen the way they stared at me and then at my essay. Then made me read aloud and I could see some of them smiling foolishly and even smirking. But I don't care; let me write on and on about them. I feel like transporting myself from here to there like the sufis did. Will write again. Just now let me pretend to sleep; otherwise, these people will go on asking useless stupid questions!

19 September—11 p.m.
Couldn't close my eyes. Can't sleep. Let me tip toe to the kitchen shed. Some little roshni/light coming from the latrine. Let me jot down all the details to our sufi dargahs. One nimazi who comes here says he brings out some Urdu risala (magazine). Maybe he can publish all these details. Yes, yes, why not! Maybe I will get some rupees from that magazine man for what I'm writing.

Okay, let me write the whole night and give it to him when he's here next. Starting off right now—Built in the pagoda style, our dargahs are laced with wooden carvings, some others equipped with bare basics. And unless there is an ongoing curfew or a crackdown in that area, you'd find many of us Kashmiris praying and even crying there. There's an emotional cum sentimental attachment of the Kashmiris with the sufis and their ziarats.

Several dargahs are situated in the Srinagar city itself. Not too far from the Nowhatta Chowk, on the banks of the Jhelum river is the dargah of Shah-i-Hamadan, who, as legends state had left the small Persian town Hamadan to escape the wrath of Timur and it is said that about seven hundred Sayyids accompanied him to the Kashmir Valley during the reign of Sultan Shihabuddin in 1372 AC. Legend also states that when Kashmiri mystic poetess Lalla Arifa saw Shah-i-Hamadan descend on the Kashmiri soil, she'd said to have uttered—at long last she had spotted a man! And the very design and architecture of this dargah stands out. At nightfall it's amazing when its reflection gets picked up by the waters of the flowing Jhelum. Though the original structure was built in 1395 it was rebuilt several times and the present structure dates back to 1732.

And near the Khanyar chowk, overlooking the main road, is the dargah of the Iraqi sufi Dastgeer sahib. The wooden architecture of this dargah carried grandeur and left an impact; but a massive fire had engulfed this dargah. Redone but not the same. Still further ahead, just few hundred metres ahead, is another ziarat with a large sized board— Ziarati Hazrati Yousa Asouph Syed Nasiruddin. Inside the compound there are two graves—one average sized but the other one far beyond the average length. And two graves are that of Hazrat Yousa Asouph and Syed Nasiruddin There are several theories around the very identity of Yousa Aza, with some of them going as far as to say he was one of the descendants of Moses.

Further ahead, on the slopes of the Hari Parbat stands the dargah of Shaikh Hamza Makhdoom, the sufi scholar of the 15 century. On the outskirts of the Srinagar city several dargahs stand out. Prominent is the dargah of the patron saint of the Kashmir Valley, Nand Rishi Sheikh Nuruddin Wali, at Charar-I-Sharief. Its original wooden structure was gutted in the mid-90s and sadly the then establishment rebuilt it with concrete and little trace of the original wooden structure. A pity that the government had re-built it with no thought whatsoever to the very history of the structure. Concrete was used, instead of wood. The concrete structure does not resemble the original structure and this had deeply hurt and upset my Kashmiris.

And several miles further is Pokhor Por. And amidst the scenic beauty, stands the dargah of the Iraqi sufi, Syed Ali. There are numerous stories about the power in command of this sufi and one of them is that even today if a man looks in the direction of the graves of the womenfolk of his family (situated on one side of the compound) he is sure to turn blind for these women were from this sufi's family and no man was supposed to see them.

20 September—1 a.m.
After nimaz and that routine daal–roti dinner, as we lay down in the room on mats, with one ceiling fan to lessen the humidity, I felt somewhat giddy. Still not getting used to eating rotis. I got up and sat in the veranda where the street throws enough light. Wanted to start writing immediately but didn't realize that the maulvis would be snoring like animals . . . that their snoring sounds would irritate me so much. They sleep in the side room, but their snores so irritating. Nah, nah, didn't want to sit near the latrine again. Very little light and too many mosquitoes. If I fall ill here, who is there to look after me. In my home all would be hovering around me. Last year when I had fever, Gulzar wouldn't leave my side, though father would keep taking him away to the other room but he would scream and get back to my side.

5 a.m.
Couldn't write more as a strange thing happened in the middle of the night. A group of four or five persons came in, from the side door. They'd come before too for the Jumma nimaz. This time they had got along a young boy, Imtiaz . . . he looked so rattled, almost fainted on the charpoy. And as they stood with a glass of water near that boy, others started sprinkling those drops on his face. I tried pushing the glass rim next to his lips, but he looked as though he was in no mood to open his mouth. 'He hit by sorrow. Just saw his abba lynched on this outer road. He also attacked, but saved. He's not speaking, not even opening his eyes. Will leave him here, safe here . . . better to be with his own people and not in their hospitals

. . . maybe those wolves catch him there and force the doctor sahibs to put some injections. Just look after him. Will recover with these children around him. We running back to the police thana!'

Yes, yes, will write again about him.

24 September—3 p.m.
Couldn't write all these days. Too much activity here. Too many people coming. Old and young men from Imtiaz's village, too scared to take him back because they say that like his father he could also be lynched and they telling us that his mother died only last month. No, she wasn't lynched by gau-rakshaks or whatever they were calling those killers but was attacked by stray dogs in their mohalla. Two or three persons came from some newspaper office, making him tell all those details—how his father was lynched and by whom? He was managing to speak but with great difficulty. And though he looked very young but told those people that he's 16 and studying in the government school of his place. He kept correcting them that his place wasn't a village but a qasbah! Don't ask me too much what's the big difference between the two but perhaps the qasbah is bigger than a village.

Will write again at night. Anyway, I sit near him in this veranda, and he's beginning to remind me of my brother Gulzar. Will write . . . there's enough light from that the street light. Maulvi sahibs have asked me to take care of him, as he also can speak little English and can understand what I am trying to say. The other boys are not my type; coming from their villages and talking only about their villages! Imtiaz knows a lot and understands what I say. No, he not like the others.

29 September—1 a.m.
I helped Imtiaz walk to the latrine. There's been silence spread around except, of course, ruptures every now and then—terrible snoring noise. Maulvis snores! He's back on the chatai (mat), walked back from the latrine himself but looking very weak. Weaker than my Gulzar. He spoke a little to me after the boys went to sleep and the maulvis had finally got off the prayer mat! His father, a hakeem, growing many herbs. But goondas wanted to grab his land and gardens, and when all their ways failed they followed his father and him coming on their scooter to Dilli, to give some of those herbs to some minister and his wife living on this road. Yes, yes,

down this big road. Those goondas attacked Imtiaz and his father right here, after accusing them of carrying beef! No, no, the minister's family didn't help. Don't ask me what happens to their land and the gardens! When I'd asked him exactly this, he started stammering . . . looking lost, crying so much.

29 September—3 a.m.

Thought I was the only one who couldn't sleep most of the night but saw Imtiaz sitting on the mat, as though talking to himself! Then he'd whispered if I could make chai for him. Of course, I could. But the maulvis could wake up and create all the hungama and start off with their silly questions—how much sugar and milk and chai-ki-patti we boiling? Or wasting, as they would say! Slowly and very slowly I made him get up and helped him walk with me to the kitchen shed under which a gas stove and utensils and the cooking bandobast is kept. All the while I was telling him that in case the maulvis wake up we should tell them that we were boiling water to clean his wounds. You know Imtiaz smiled and smiled at that! Yes, he did, although he in great pain.

30 September—2 a.m.

Been waiting for Imtiaz to come this side and we make chai like last night. But he's not getting up, although I have been throwing paper balls at his feet. Anyway, let me keep on writing, so much to tell you about this boy. He knows so much, not like these other boys. All silly duffers! This Imtiaz told me that plant leaves are the best medicines—Jamun leaves for some disorder called diabetes, Guava leaves for colds and coughs, Bel and Pudina leaves for stomach upset, Neem leaves for skin boils and rashes and yes, he told that they were also supplying Mehndi leaves to that minister's wife for her hair and also for her friends. He kept telling me in great detail that all old women use Mehndi leaves to colour their hair. I told him I also want those leaves for my mother and grandmother. Told him to get those leaves. Suddenly he started looking very tense and kept telling me he wants to run back to his gardens and look after those trees. No, he didn't look scared to get back. Kept saying he's missing his trees and lands and if he does not get back all those village people and the police will enter his place and take it all up!

30 September—3 a.m.

He still not up. How to make tea? Also, want to also ask him how he plans to run away from here. I also want to get going from here. Just can't become a bank clerk if I stay here. And all these mosquitoes! And the rash all over my neck and head not going. Yesterday this maulvi kept on putting the topi right back on my head even when I told him that there are boils. He wasn't one bit bothered even when I told him I am running to the latrine ten times a day! Not sure whether the maulvi dials my toth's number or some wrong number. How is it that his mobile doesn't ring! Not ringing for so many days. Hope toth hasn't sold it off like mouj had done. I want to run back, but Imtiaz told me that this hundred rupee note with me will take me just till the bus stop. Then what! What about running away with Imtiaz to his place. At least all the leaves will settle my stomach and I will not have to wear this topi all day!

1 October—3.30 p.m.

Busy all day. Been my turn to cut the onions and grind the garlic–ginger–pudina chutney on the sill-batta. Then, that Quraishi qasai came for his nimaz and before leaving he took out a small packet wrapped in so many layers and layers of akhbars/newspaper sheets, and out came some chicken pieces. The boys looked so happy and more than them the maulvis. Shakeel made qorma, and you should have seen how they kept dipping the fat rotis into the shorba-salan.

The big thing that happened after they ate is that all went to lie down but Imtiaz and I sat in the kitchen shed—I washing the utensils, all the pateelas and bartans, and he talking to me . . . very, very softly. He told me of his big plan to get going from here. Will write again, as time for the early evening nimaz and just got to say it, otherwise you know the maulvis start off about Jannat and Dozakh!

1 October—7 p.m.

Imtiaz told me he knows where the minister lives. Not too far from this madrasa. I have to take him there, and he will try to meet that minister or his wife. How to take him there! How? Somehow! He a very clever boy and told me that tomorrow is Mahatma Gandhi's birthday, so a big holiday, and minister sahib and his wife will be home and all that he has to do is to meet them. He telling me that how happy that minister janab and his begum sahiba were with his abba, as his abba was giving them all sorts of leaves and flower extracts for their health problems... I know I will have to tell maulvi sahib that I want to take Imtiaz to Khan Market but not too sure whether we'll get permission because he could be once again attacked by the goondas.

Now this Imtiaz been calling me to the kitchen side but that maulvi is standing right there, looking all too excited. Don't know why? Okay, okay, there comes that man with an old fridge. Yes, last Jumma this same man was telling us that he going to Qatar to work in a school but before going he'll give his old fridge for us.

10 p.m.

So much excitement for this fridge! So old and used it looks. What will maulvis keep in it? Maybe plastic jugs of water. Worried whether I'll be able to take Imtiaz out of this place. Just tried to talk to him while the others were 'welcoming' the fridge, but he was so busy rubbing the Neem paste on the wounds on his hands and legs, and then got carried away, detailing all the miracles to the Neem leaves. Imagine, telling that old teacher to carry Neem leaves all the way to Qatar! I have an idea—why don't I talk right away to maulvi sahib about the Khan Market going. He is looking so excited, he'll give permission.

3 October—4 p.m.

'Hell! Hell it's been! Don't know what more hellish stuff will happen here. Just hope they don't tear away my diary . . . let me write as much as I can, before I get thrown out. No idea where to! Look at the way these maulvis are trying my father's mobile from early morning. They want to throw me back. Good. I want to get back. But suppose they don't get through then what. They can put me in the bus to my Kashmir and I will reach home. Try and take along Imtiaz but he doesn't want to go to my Kashmir. Only and only thinking of his lands in his Uttar or Ulta Pradesh as he calls it! Thought he's clever but what a useless plan he'd come up with. Now hate him. Can you imagine how risky it got to lie here to the maulvi sahib that we going till Khan Market. Only gave permission if we took four other boys for Imtiaz's safety. Took us one hour to search that big minister's house, as Imtiaz went looking at those big iron gates, foolishly staring at those name plates. Finally when he spotted that big house, the security chaps looked at us as though we've landed from some enemy country!

They didn't seem bothered about monkeys swaying just above their heads on the Neem tree branches but looked at us as though each one of us was carrying a dagger! I think one of them did recognize Imtiaz when he told them that minister sahib and his begum sahib used to meet him and his father, when they'd got along all those herbs and leaves, but he was made to shut up. They decided to not just question us but even throw us back to where we walked from—our madrasa! Imagine, throwing us into a jeep and then throwing us to these maulvis. One of them questioning the maulvis for keeping me here—I can't get over his words—'You people keeping an atankwadi here. He could become a terrorist! Throw him back to Kashmir. Throw him out before we shut your ISIS factory!'

5 October—11 a.m.
Don't know how much to write or not write! Surely I will get sent off from here. Today or tomorrow. No, not to my Kashmir. Many persons coming here for discussions with the maulvis. They tried my toth's mobile number but saying it's not working. That old boy here, Shakeel telling me that all these persons are managing the madrasa and keep sending what they call galla anaaj, for making the daal and rotis. He whispering these men take all the decisions. Don't know where they throwing me from here. They look so scared of the police here. I could see the old maulvi's hands shaking when that fellow was scolding him for keeping me—a Kashmiri!

5 October—5 p.m.
They did not listen to me when I kept crying that I want to get back home, somehow or anyhow! I just don't want to get thrown about to new places!

5 October—10 p.m.
Not eaten a thing. Don't want to. Though these boys gathered around me, saying that I shouldn't sleep hungry. Yes, feeling hungry but can't even think of having rotis. Don't know what happens tomorrow. Will they really send me off or are they going to keep me back. Couldn't complete what I wanted to say . . . Maulvis called me towards the kitchen side; maybe because they didn't want the other children to hear us. They looked tense. Telling me that they will be sending me to a madrasa in Muzaffarnagar. And they have called some people from there to take me along with them. Like a fool I thought they are sending me to our Kashmir's Muzaffarabad,

but when I told them I'm okay about going to Muzaffarabad, they were about to slap me, shrieking—'You Kashmiris! No, it's not your Muzaffarabad but our Muzaffarnagar in our Uttar Pradesh. Nor very far from here but can't send you alone. Wait, till those men from there will reach'. These maulvis did not even want to hear any of my pleas to get going to Kashmir. Raising their voice, they kept saying—'Who on earth will want to take you from here to your Kashmir—to be called all sorts of names, to be thrown in some rotten qaidkhaana (prison)!'

6 October—3 a.m.

Been sitting, staring all around. Running to the latrine and then even going somewhat out of here, from the side gate to the side lane. Got back, too scared as those ministers' houses not too far. One of the boundary walls right here, camouflaged with lots of trees and shrubs. You know what, I could see the branches laden with red *Anaars* on that wall. Felt too scared to pluck out even one *Anaar* although that would have been best for my upset stomach. Suddenly I remembered this verse of our Kashmiri poet Maqbul Shah Kralawari:

> The pomegranate trees are full of red flowers,
> The nightingale took them to be on fire,
> And flew away.
> The verdure was spread like a carpet of green velvet,
> Whereupon petals of flowers were scattering gold and silver coins.
> The red and white and yellow petals were falling
> Scattering gold and silver on violet beds.
> And innumerable were the fruit trees,
> Fragrant and shady willows.

7 October—8 a.m.

A lot of hustle–bustle since dawn, when I woke up for the fajr nimaz. One auto rickshaw halted and out came three maulvis—all wearing creamy-coloured (white turned creamy!) pathan suits and with long beards. Here to take me with them to their madrasa. I stood near the kitchen shed, seeing the boys frying eggs for them and after weeks parathas were being made with oil dripping. Imtiaz was also around, he neared and continued whispering—telling me he knows that madrasa where they're sending me

. . . not too far from his lands and gardens. And he will come to meet me there and also get me out of there. I gave him a dirty look! Before I could glare any further, little Abuzair neared and lisped that those maulvis wanted to meet me.

7 October—11 a.m.

Those maulvis sitting in a row. Looking at me as though I was a lifafa (papery packet) to be transported from here to there. Short of saying I'd be packed off towards Jannat, they went on to assure or re-assure me in hugely flowery Urdu words and sentences which went above my head, that I would be going to safer place, as that madrasa is situated in a place where there are many Muslims living all around. They also added that even Imtiaz would be getting packed off with me. As one of the maulvis muttered—'here too many police wallahs coming because of you and him. Too much tension. There it will be less of these musibats. Don't want this madrasa to be attacked and destroyed, like they did to our Babri masjid!'

3

Around the Plains of North India

14 October—2 a.m.

Writing after so many days. How could I write any earlier! What a horrible journey in a bus, and then when the bus broke down we were stuffed in a tempo, and then finally in a rickshaw as the tempo couldn't enter the narrow lanes and by-lanes to this new madrasa where I now sit stuffed. Don't know what the hell those Dilli maulvis were telling me about this place, as though it's going to be nothing short of Jannat for me. Even reaching this place took hours; although they were saying Muzaffarnagar is only two or three hours from Dilli. It took us many hours. Just see the sweat trickling down but no water to even wash my face. These people living in their eighteenth century world!

I've realized that Imtiaz is totally correct when he keeps mumbling that nobody can beat your qismat! Imagine, me born in my Srinagar but rotting in this dust . . . getting thrown from one place to the next. I really wanted to shut that old maulvi when he'd kept looking at my face and muttering that keeping me, a Kashmiri, will sure to get the whole madrasa into trouble! He should have had me thrown back to my home but look where I landed!

Imtiaz also looks shocked here, but he could somehow eat those thick-thick rotis and that watery daal and now sleeps but I can't. Want to run away but how to! At least in that Dilli madrasa, there was some hope of getting back home but here all hopes dashed for me. Sabr and sabr and sabr is what I'm trying to keep but no use!

Will write again. I think the maulvi is up . . . woken up in the middle of the night for saying his *tahajjud nimaz* and might come this side and ask me what I'm scribbling away.

4 a.m.—Fellow kept on praying non-stop, and now I can hear him snoring. Don't ask me how these 40 children are sleeping with that maulvi's snores echoing all over. I have now moved towards the kitchen space which

The Diary of Gull Mohammad. Humra Quraishi, Oxford University Press. © Oxford University Press India 2023.
DOI: 10.1093/oso/9789391050269.003.0004

opens towards the inner lane where the tube light flickers. I don't know why they've made half the courtyard as some sort of a kitchen when all that gets cooked here is rotis and daal and chai and more chai . . . in this entire one week that I have been here nothing else been cooked, though those two boys from Assam, Rahil and Rahmat, told me that earlier gosht was also cooked but last month after many goondas had entered this madrasa, beat up the maulvi, accusing him of cooking gau-maas, there has been a complete halt to meat-cooking.

You know they also said that instead of the thanedar or that daroga catching those goondas those cops beat up the maulvi sahib and nobody could say a word . . . that maulvi sahib was also from Assam and left. They also been telling me that he didn't go back to Assam, but to some other nearby madrasa. They saying he can't go back to Assam as his name is not in some big fat 'citizenship-register' so he will be thrown off into Bangladesh. This, when his children's names are there in that register, but he will be thrown off. Strange nah!

Don't know where the hell will I be thrown off from here! Don't know what's going to happen to my head if I stay here any longer! Whenever I have tried to talk to Imtiaz about we running away to his home he looks all too worked up and worried. Tomorrow I just have to talk to him, maybe around afternoon when this maulvi goes for his nap and the boys are sent off to sweep the compound and water the creepers.

Funny this maulvi goes nowhere, not even till the lane. Nah, nah, he is not from Assam. These boys are saying he's been here only very recently after the other maulvi left all too suddenly. This one is originally from Bihar but many years back his people shifted to this state. You know most of the security creatures near my Srinagar home were from Bihar but didn't look like this maulvi sahib. They too ferocious looking and this chap all too meek.

15 October—11 p.m. Today got to know the reason for Imtiaz's changed behaviour. He is telling me that the *mahaul* here and around his home place is very bad, he saying that never before the Musalmaans of this place faced this sort of hate atmosphere against them. The older boys saying that many goondas have been barging in, picking up fights with the maulvi on what's cooking or not cooking. Even when daal is getting cooked they accuse him of cooking gau-maas! They also said that earlier the maulvi sahib used to take these children to the local cricket grounds to play cricket but last

month those goondas had caught hold of maulvi sahib and threatened and abused him. They even tried to throw off maulvi sahib's skull cap. Too scary!

Who are these goondas that these boys talk of? They telling me these goondas can attack and can beat us madrasa children very, very badly. Why? Because we are Musalmaans and look Musalmaans because of our kurtas and topis, and these goondas hate Musalmaans just like an enemy does, so much so that they get proper training in killing us. These boys are not sure whether they can kidnap us too! You know in my Srinagar, my mother and father used to sit worrying, scared that Gulzar could be kidnapped and then trained into guns and all that fighting. Poor Gulzar so weak, can never imagine him to be a gun fighter but father used to keep muttering that kidnappers are forever on the lookout for such children who are weak and can never free themselves from their clasp.

Silly of me to keep thinking of my home, my people, when destiny has thrown me here. Silly, bloody stupid place where one can't even step out. I have to talk to Imtiaz again . . . want to run away from here with him. Just wait till the morning and will force him to run out of this madrasa.

20 October—11 p.m. or maybe 11.30 p.m.
Shukar Allah! Am alive and my limbs not pulled apart. These last five days have been hell and will continue to be hell. That night when I was cursing my fate and was making plans to run out of that madrasa, it was attacked and we had run for our lives. Maulvi sahib fractured his leg while trying to run and tripped. Many men with lathis and revolvers in their hands caught hold of him but even as he was crying in pain he was telling us to run towards the outer mohallas. Nobody knows what's happened to maulvi sahib—many are saying that he was killed there and then, others saying he was dragged and then thrown somewhere in that drain that flows near that outer road. Several shrieking that he's been cooking gau-maas in the madrasa.

Madrasa children and I are alive because we could run very fast, so not caught by those horrible looking men carrying big, big lathis and what not! But by the time we could reach this outer mohalla—homes were burning. All that I could get to see were flames and women and men running with their children. We also ran with them till the big road where so many trucks and cars were passing by. No, not one driver halted to ask hundreds of us what's wrong; why those hysterical shrieks of women and children.

We sat with them on the edge of that road and the entire night passed by. Morning some police wallahs came and also some other sarkari people and one minister who said that tents will be put up till the situation is made to turn normal.

For me, it was the first time to have seen this sort of mad frenzy getting unleashed. Even children were not spared. The entire night Imtiaz just gazed at the stars and moon, just about muttering repeatedly, 'How many more times will we Musalmaans be made to sit like refugees in our own land!' Without me asking him any details, he kept muttering, telling me how he has seen so many riots, right from the time he could see and sense. I told him I could no longer hear all those details of how his two uncles were tied to an electric pole and their heads dashed against the pole or else how his grandfather's farmhouse was burnt by the local mafia who were close to the police wallahs. My head had begun to pain and I almost shut my eyes and my ears. But he went on, as though coming up with an unending sort of eerie lullaby for himself!

I couldn't sleep! What sleep . . . no sleep . . . mosquitoes and cries and the uncertainty of what would lie ahead with dawn making way.

Morning got along nothing much except chai and a whole lot of chatter. Several women collected twigs and tree branches lying around and put a twisted degchi or container overflowing with water collected from the nearby tube well and put the water on boil, adding chai-patti (tea leaves) and gur (jaggery) and then stirring the concoction rather too mechanically. In that same emotionless way pouring it in cracked saucers. Some drank it, others looked about hopelessly and shook their necks rather nervously like semi-rusted pendulums. I looked at Imtiaz as he tried to hold a saucer overflowing with that concoction and sipping it with much effort. As though a formality had to be completed, before getting up all too suddenly and announcing that it's time we go find the maulvi sahib.

It's then we got the shock of our lives—several around told us that maulvi wouldn't have been left alive, and we would also meet the same fate if we dare go back. Danga, danga they kept saying where the police is helping the local mafia headed by one big goonda Somi Sikka and his partner Mukka Hero.

Then what! Nothing! Kept sitting on the edge of this road—some called it highway. By afternoon some police wallahs came with two men clad in white, said to be mantri sahib and his son. One of the wrinkled women squatting near me with her grandchildren cried out that her son is not to be found and then she caught hold of mantri's white sandals, begging him that her son be traced. He simply kicked her and her pleas and addressed the uprooted us in a stone like emotion-less voice—'Tents and more tents will be put up . . . live in those. Don't even dare go back. Can't protect you all. Don't you all want to be left alive? Then sit inside tents!'

Shrieks and howls took over. There seemed nothing much to say or hear. And in the next couple of hours, plastic or nylon or polyester sheets or rolls were thrown towards us. And then after another two hours a truck offloaded wooden sticks to take on the weight of those sheets!

By now several other madrasa children sat close to where Imtiaz and I sat. They whispered that they were going to walk back to the madrasa to collect their clothes and other belongings and also to see if maulvi sahib was alive. Suddenly, Imtiaz sat up all too charged, all too worked up— 'What about our Separaas, our Quran Paak . . . all to be got from there . . . cannot be left there. Don't know what these police wallahs will do to our madrasa and to our things!'

Though he was in that surcharged mood to get going that very second, Talib, the oldest and wisest madrasa student amongst us, pulled him back, whispering that we have got to remove our skull caps and also our kurta pyjamas—'from a distance we madrasa students stand out and those goondas will catch and roast us alive. We go back only in our vests and shorts. We don't go together but only in twos and threes.'

Somehow I felt the entire plan to be very risky, but I decided to go along with the boys because my diaries were there in my bag left back in that madrasa. I wasn't one bit bothered about the clothes, and if wasn't for the diaries, I wouldn't have decided to get back.

Slowly we started moving somewhat away from the crowds along the road and more towards the bushes and trees. Nobody even bothered to ask us any of the usual queries—why or where to? Obviously, all too caught up with their survival, with the mess getting messier. Imtiaz and I went towards the Babool bushes, undressing to the extent of throwing away the kurtas and the topis. I had to keep my pyjamas on, as I wore no underwear; never did possess one. I took off the topi and the semi-torn kurta. Imtiaz threw aside every cloth piece on him except for the under-wear. We saw three older boys quietly walking across the trees and then walking still ahead.

Imtiaz looked nervously towards me and said that we should wait for the evening to set in and then it would be somewhat safer as nobody would recognize us, but though I kept telling him that by evening all our stuff in that madrasa would be stolen or burnt, so either now or never, but, yes, nervous I was . . . more so, as he'd once again started muttering how his uncles were killed by lathi yielding men and how his other relatives been recounting the horrors of rioting. Suddenly he looked all too rattled and coming close to my face uttered the very obvious, 'You look so very Kashmiri! Those devils and the police wallahs will sure to catch you immediately, with or without pyjamas! You silly boy!'

But my diaries . . . my copies and books?

'You talking of books! You going to be torn apart and your books will be thrown in that drain. You going crazy! Don't go back. By now they would have burnt our madrasa and killed many more. You haven't see what maar–kaat–dhaar takes place here! Too much violence.'

The dilemma and the obvious danger of getting back, weighing on my nerves but before I could take the next step forwards or backwards, two or three big-bodied vehicles halted on the main road, with the crowds chanting that phoren media and Dilli patrakaars (journalists) had come to visit the mohallas, the madrasa and the nearly villages. Then suddenly several police vehicles and also the DM and SDM cars also stopped.

The journalists and officers walking towards the strife-torn villages and mohallas and then perhaps towards our madrasa. I told Imtiaz that it was our chance—our only and only chance—to get going with them. He nodded, at least with these patrakaars around those goondas would not be allowed to kill or loot; so, yes, somewhat safe.

Half-clad or one could say semi-clad we kept walking, with me covering my face with the semi-torn kurta. My chappals were unable to take the strain of the rough rocky terrain and midway I threw them aside. In the usual course, Imtiaz would have commented, but not today. He looked very tense as we walked, trying to maintain some distance from the group that was walking ahead rather too briskly. After all, they had leathery boots or walking shoes on their feet. My feet absolutely naked.

Suddenly the group seemed to halt rather too abruptly—they had spotted a bearded man's body floating in that drain?

I looked at Imtiaz and whispered rather too nervously, 'Could be our maulvi sahib?'

He nodded and then kept nodding, till shrieks intruded. Several villagers had recognized our maulvi sahib's dead body. Complete confusion overtook, as the cops tried to shoo away the villagers and at the same time tried to maintain 'law and order'. Journalists took pictures, even as the officers tried to explain to them that if those pictures get splashed it could add to the communal surcharged atmosphere. One amongst the journalists raised her voice and told the sarkari sahibs that what more communal madness can take place when bodies of old maulvis can be seen floating around!

Suddenly Imtiaz pulled me aside and asked me to run towards the madrasa before the police and the media lands there to gather more information on the poor maulvi sahib. We ran, took the side track, which led to the Guava orchards and then further towards the madrasa.

Our madrasa's side wall lay broken and the front gate twisted and burnt. Though the interiors seemed somewhat untouched, expect the kitchen shed was broken and the daal-galla-anaaj (food grain) gone from the several kanastars. Imtiaz and I rushed inwards to stuff our clothes and copies and books into the bags. By now two other boys, Maaz and Mateen, had reached and were standing sobbing as their clothes were not to be found—they had probably left them on the Neem tree branches to get dried. Nah, no time to look around for clothes. We tried to rush out and go back to the highway along the same route but the police and the rest of the team were coming this way through the orchards. For minutes we stood frightened, especially I, as I saw one of the sipahis (cops) staring at my face as though he seemed to have sensed that I was a Kashmiri, but then, after all those stares he turned attention towards the fruit-laden trees.

3.30 a.m.

Sitting once again under the highway tube light, scribbling away rather too hurriedly whenever I can snatch time. At times two paragraphs, at times not even two lines or even two words.

Nobody has been sleeping around. Mosquitoes and the smell from the open drains getting unbearable. But Imtiaz seems too scared to move from here, not even till the Guava orchards to gather fruit.

Many families sat huddled under the government distributed tents, but for the last one day, nobody has eaten a thing. Yes, tea is made by putting water into a container lookalike, which is put atop a cluster of burning twigs, then gur added to the boiling water and that concoction circulated around. Some women put chopped guavas with gur, boiling and stirring the concoction till a lovely smell spread around. And though we looked rather too longingly towards that mixture, but it was distributed only among their children.

Last evening I'd suddenly burst out, crying for food but all I got were stares and those loud enough whispers from those hanging around, with several of them even asking Imtiaz whether I was from Kashmir, but Imtiaz was smart enough to say I'm a Pahari!

And these semi-starved if not fully-starved people believed this, several even coming up with those typical offshoots, '*Pahari! Yeh Garhwal ka hai ya Uttarakhand ka hai?*' (From the mountains! Is he from Garhwal or from Uttarakhand?)

'*Nah . . . nah, yeh Himachali!*' (No... he is Himachali, from Himachal.)

'*Theek hai. Shukar Allah yeh ladka Kashmiri nahin hai, nahin toh daroga-jee paagal ho jatai. Hum sab ko jail qaid kar daitai!*' (Thank God! He is not from Kashmir, otherwise the daroga would have been too upset, would have us all jailed!)

Can't say what's going to happen to me, to my very survival in this strange setup. Never in their dreams could my parents or grandparents visualized that I'd be surviving in this way, where I'll be all too frightened to reveal my Kashmiri identity. These other boys don't have that Kashmir tag to them. They just have the Muslim tag to them, but with me it's Kashmiri Muslim and that becomes so very lethal that I'm called Pahari and not Kashmiri! Why the hell Kashmiris are so hated here! When we spotted tourists in my Srinagar we didn't look at them with hatred. So many women in saris and bindis and all those other clothes like jeans but not one of them looked scared of us Kashmiris.

But why is it that I am always so scared here. At times I get this terrible urge to paint my face all grey or black or brown. Perhaps, would have even done so if I had all those colours . . . paint boxes with me.

You know when I'd first entered the madrasa in this place, maulvi sahib had taken Imtiaz and me aside and told us in a firm way that nobody should be told that I am from Kashmir. He looked at me so very sternly that I couldn't pick up the courage to ask him the 'why' to it but as we stood there all too quiet he himself added some sort of an explanation—'Very difficult times here for us Musalmaans. Police keeping a watch on us, on our madrasa, who comes and lives here. Keeping you here is a big risk, as goondas are looking for excuses to attack us.'

Imtiaz had kept nodding to each one of the long and short utterances. Maulvi sahib had even gone into the bygones—telling me details to the targeted attacks that had taken place in this very area in 2013 . . . he detailing how hundreds were finished for life, forced to run from their ancestral homes, shivering and dying in tents. Imtiaz had tears running down his cheeks and what startled me is the way he told maulvi to stop coming up with more details. He had to, as just then, two men had come to take us—the madrasa children—to their village home for 'Quran Khwani' (recitation of the Quran). We had to keep on chanting the verses from the Quran for hours. Then came the food—daal and rotis and halwa. One of the men whose house it was, telling us that his farm lands were set on fire in the 2013 Muzffarnagar riots by the political mafia. He had also kept saying that earlier he would have qorma and kebabs cooked but not in this mahaul where mantris can eat chicken and mutton, but Musalmaans have to be so very careful even while cooking cabbage and potatoes!

21 October—Don't know the exact time—ending of the night. I am scribbling away under this tube light, somewhat not too far from the tents.

Oh Allah, what's happening to me! Dying to eat just something. Were they not saying that not too far from here there are several dhabas, those roadside eateries, where truckers and cars stop and we could take up some sort of work there—at least to fill our stomachs if nothing else.

I wanted to start walking immediately, but these boys pulled me back. Said we should wait till the morning and then start off.

Don't know whether I will even get a truck cleaner's job—what with my Kashmiri looks. Unless one of the truckers is a Kashmiri, but I'm not born with such luck, otherwise I wouldn't be sitting here with mosquitoes trying to squeeze blood from my veins, with so many hungry children sitting and crying all around.

Daybreak . . . sun out but not really shining.

Though I want to keep writing, look at the way all these people staring at me, with one of them even just passing snide comments—'Bhaiyya Pahari! Kya collector banne ke khwab dekh rahe ho!' (Brother Pahari, dreaming of becoming a collector or what!)

In this tense mahaul, they are sitting wondering what the hell I could be scribbling away. I paused, only to see Imtiaz and those three other boys sitting blankly, resting their back against the huge Neem trees. Two other boys of the madrasa came nearer towards me, muttering that police allowed us to move back and stay in the madrasa but these other men are saying that it's not safe. Better to be altogether here. If we go back, the killers of maulvi sahib will kill us too.

But before that we could die of hunger.

9 a.m.—for the last two hours or so, I'd been sitting with Imtiaz and the other boys and nobody has an answer to what's next. And what do we eat?

Even if we trace those supposed dhabas who will pay for rotis. Those dhaba men could shoo us away and then what!

Been tempted to ask the two elderly women for some bits of rotis with them, but they seem much too preoccupied minding their grandchildren while the rest of the clan—men and women—lie crumpled on the mats. No, they wouldn't shoo me off nor snarl at me . . . there's a certain kindness on their faces. But what if they all too suddenly ask me whether I'm a Kashmiri! No, I'll not be able to call myself Pahari! I'd rather be stabbed to death. Stopping here. Very hungry and thirsty, feeling so weak!

24 October

Hell . . . ongoing hell! My this diary somewhat soaked in these waters but will try and put it in the sun. Wait, sabr, the sun will be out. Sabr, but don't know whether I will get to put it so very openly as I saw these two women collecting twigs and scraps of paper to burn; just in case they tear it off and burn up the pages. No, no! These two women whom I thought were kind spoke like wretches to Alamgir—the four-year-old left in our madrasa only last week. Don't know whether he's from Bengal or Assam, but can't speak Hindustani. He keeps crying for his father who'd left him at the madrasa. Imtiaz saying that this child's family is living in some camp in Assam as the police has given them some days to show their papers; the poor father been leaving all his children here and there. Don't ask me what papers, to prove what! Imtiaz gave me those strange looks as though I'm some dumb creature, when I had asked him what papers, papers for what? He screamed on my face—citizenship papers to show that they are Indians and not from Bangladesh! Then he screaming more unsettling stuff, 'Can't say how true it is but they saying that this sarkar will start something like this in here, in this pradesh. Where are those papers with us where my abbajaan or his abbajaan came from! Nobody asking us how they got murdered, by whom!'

Alamgir's crying not stopping. His nose red, eyes swollen, hair matted. He's been looking all around for his father. He was left back by his father like I was left back. But I am much older, so I can cope with the pain and shocks. He can't. It looks that he might die. Better to die quickly and not slowly like I'm dying here.

No, I haven't forgotten single detail of my home, of my people, but these people don't want me to even utter the word—Kashmir. They look all too rattled and give me those look as though I should be having some sense in me, as though they will be all shot dead or something as disastrous if the others discover that there's a Kashmiri in their midst.

Don't know how long we will sit like this. At night it gets cold . . . in fact, very cold but then what to do. Couldn't write earlier but two days back, when Imtiaz and several other boys did go back to the madrasa there was nothing in there, even the side walls broken into, the whole place looked completely vandalized. When I had walked in there, clasping Alamgir's hand, I couldn't stand still. Too shocked to see the complete destruction of the madrasa. And though one or two men from the village Karva told us that we could stay there but there seemed little point. Plus the danger of getting attacked, so got back to this roadside tent, which is torn and breaking apart.

Another very upsetting thing, the diary pages are getting loose, more so lately as I have been tucking it under my kurta for fear of it getting stolen by these women and men around, for burning fire.

And in all this mess I'm looking for more pages that I could stick to this diary. You know the last 20 pages were stuck last week, in that madrasa by maulvi sahib himself. Nah, no glue in that madrasa. Just a quick paste made out of well-kneaded atta, and with that those pages duly stuck on the last page of my diary. That poor maulvi had helped me put those pages together with that atta paste.

Poor maulvi sahib now dead and so very quickly buried—well, as quickly as he had stuck those pages! If alive he would have been also sitting here with us, hungry and angry and would have been talking of the communal attacks in this Muzaffarnagar region. Poor maulvi sahib never spoke of his family. Once or twice I had asked him about his children but he looked the other way, with the older boys, Tariq and Tahir, later telling us that his only son was killed by Hindutva brigades in riots, and after that he and his wife moved to some relative's home in Karva village, where his wife died because of too many vomits and he moved into the madrasa.

I'd thought only my Kashmiris getting killed but here I have seen so much of death and destruction. All these men, women and children are talking only and only of death and how to survive the upcoming winter. Don't know what's to happen tomorrow.

25 October—6 a.m.—I woke up very, very early as I could hear a mobile ring loud and clear next to my ear . . . Anyway, it's that half sleep sort of sleep, what with all of us huddled under tents.

Though several men are carrying mobiles with them but not using them because batteries are either failing or fading or there's no connectivity. Two or three days back I'd rather too hesitatingly asked Asghar sahib—yes that man with that long beard who is said to be the main qasai (butcher) of the village, but now he's been looking for grass-blades or grass to cook after he was accused of selling cow meat and his butchery set on fire by Sanghis as he insists or persists on calling them—if I could use his mobile to call my family. With that request he looked all too rattled and asked me the number so that he would himself dial and just as I was about to mutter my toth's number, Imtiaz pinched my arm and told Asghar sahib that he shouldn't dial for me as my family would only get too upset. Angrily I almost pounced on him even as he kept whispering 'You crazy, he'll know you're from Kashmir. From the number won't he know! And then hell. The whole camp will know. Another musibat on our heads!'

My sobbing made little difference. Imagine, I haven't heard their voices for months now. Suddenly I couldn't even sob freely as screams and shrieks overtook. Asghar sahib's sister was said to be delivering a baby. We were told to move further away, perhaps making sure that we wouldn't even get to glance in that direction. Though we did move further, but those screams and shrieks could be heard for many hours. Then all too suddenly a baby's wail pierced through!

29 October—9 p.m.
This time writing, sitting atop a boulder, on the roadside. We have moved somewhat away from the tents, though not very far. The streetlight is on and while these three other boys are sitting huddled on a bag, I found a boulder. Let's see till when can I write . . . feeling weak and hungry.

The situation in that tented setup had been worsening, with the nights getting colder and the burning bandobast lessening. Also lesser gur and atta supplies to keep us physically alive.

Pulling me aside, Imtiaz told me that now we have only two options— either run towards his village or else run towards another nearby village where there are a large number of masjids—we stay there before we sit here dying of hunger and cold.

What about the dhabas? The minute they heard the word dhaba these boys told me some terrible dirty stuff about the characters hanging around the dhabas! *Chakkas*, they kept calling them. Don't know why I kept arguing with them. Looking disgusted and just too fed up with my stubborn insistence, they told me that it would be okay to see for my-self . . . we could be passing those dhabas if we walked along the main highway.

I wanted to take along Alamgir, but Imtiaz's impatience was so obvious. He started calling me all sorts of names, saying that Alamgir's crying would land us in severe trouble. Though the older three boys, Waseem, Kareem, and Naseem, agreed with him, but wouldn't leave back Alamgir. They decided to stay back though till the end looked unsure of their decision.

I looked at Alamgir and wanted to stay back too but Imtiaz kept telling me that this was my only chance to get going, if nowhere else then at least till his family orchards and lands. Later we could come back and see how many more boys from here can be taken with us. His one sentence hitting—they are from here but you are the only one from your Kashmir! Be careful otherwise you'd be lynched. . . goondas roaming around!

30 October—11 p.m. or maybe around midnight
Around afternoon, four of us—Imtiaz, Sohail, Sultan, and I—finally decided to walk down the highway, without our skull caps. Walking , by the side of the highway. This big wide road leading us where . . . nowhere!

Will write again as no energy left to write. So exhausted. Let me recover somewhat. Don't even know the exact time—no watches on us.

Before starting Imtiaz had asked one of the men around that highway, the date or the day. Couldn't have queried any further as there could have been counter-queries thrown at us.

2 November—very late night

After we'd walked for many minutes, maybe for 40 minutes, a row of dhabas stood out. There was dirt and water flooding the area but nothing seemed to come in way as the smell of food held sway. Saliva dripping from the side of my mouth. We stood staring at one of the dhabas where jalebis were getting deep fried at one end and thick parathas made at the other end. I looked at the boys, but before I could say a thing Imtiaz took out a soiled ten rupee note tucked inside the *tahveez* hung ever so loyally around his neck. 'I have only this with me . . . what about you all?' We looked blank.

The dhaba fellow sensed our penniless condition. His scowling somewhat abated as Imtiaz walked up to him and asked him to give jalebis and parathas for those ten rupees. That man laughed like a hyena and said with that money we'll get only one paratha and four jalebis; which he placed on a twisted aluminium plate. Within seconds the four of us tore the paratha into bits and just too greedily ate the jalebis. But hunger pangs only increased, so much so that I asked that same man if we could do some work in the dhaba and in return get some food. He nodded and went to ask a huge looking man—perhaps the owner—and then came scowling back, asking for our names. Hearing our names, screaming—*'Musalmaan ho . . . bhago yahan se . . . miya logon kee dukaan mai jaoo. Musalmaano ka yahan koi kaam nahin.'* (You all Muslims. Run away from here. Go towards shops run by Muslims. Not here. Muslims not needed here!)

Even as we tried walking away, I could hear him throw taunts at us. We walked till the end of the row of dhabas but no Muslim-looking owner could be seen. Just then saw a rickshaw cart pulled along by a Muslim-looking bearded old man. We stopped him only to ask if he knew of any dhaba run by a Muslim. He shook his head in a strangely sapped way and said that after the 2013 communal rioting Muslims moved away from this area and opened some eateries in other small towns and villages. But he added that he knew of one 'good Hindu' who runs a small hotel at the other end of the road. Maybe he could keep us for washing utensils but not for cooking. While he was giving out details to him, Imtiaz fell down, fainted . . . we tried to explain to that dazed looking cart puller that we all were trying to walk and talk without water or food for hours, save those bits plucked out from that one lone paratha and four jalebis. He helped us put Imtiaz in that cart and carted him, with the three of us following him through the narrow lanes. Finally, before all of us could faint he parked his cart near a one room structure and the first thing he did was to keep throwing water on Imtiaz's neck and head and face. While he was doing so, an old woman with an equally old looking dupatta on her frail shoulders came out of the dwelling. She must have been the same age of my grandmother but while she'd looked well built (at least that's what she looked when I last saw her) but this lady looked too haggard and bent . . . too old to be this cart puller's wife. She turned out to be his mother, as he kept calling her amma, while pulling out a charpoy and making Imtiaz sit on it. Imtiaz had opened his eyes but looked much too drained out to even utter a word. The cart puller dragged a water container, which he'd called 'ghara', near us and told us to drink as much water as we could. Saying that unlike other areas where there's not a drop of water to drink, here no problem as there's an old well in the backyard. Then he'd made his mother take out gur and laiyya (puffed rice) from the big kanastars and gave us to eat. When his mother tried to say something about rotis he vetoed her suggestions, snubbing her rather too openly—'You know you can't make more than four rotis . . . they are very hungry, dropping dead. Quickly make some khichri and chutney. Our Musalmaan children . . . where can they go!' Turning his attention back on us, he repeated, 'Before the 2013 dangas many, many Muslim families were here but now only we here and one zamindar sahib and that's all. All gone! I would have also left this place if had biwi and bacchas to protect from these goondas around. Didn't marry so no wife and children with me.'

Will write again. Don't know when . . . as the papers and the pen are getting over and feeling so very weak that can't describe.

Been writing all this from cart puller Ramzana's dwelling. There's been ample light. Don't know the exact time but late night—you could say very late night!

4 November—11 p.m.
Finally got with me a proper thick note book and a new pen and also a haveli roof on my head!

Strange but true!

Writing all those details. One by one.

I want to write the whole night. Don't know when next I can write with this sort of peace spread around.

That night after we gulped down that khichri, we slept in the court-yard. And though there were stray dogs loitering around but that cart puller—Ramzana —kept telling us that these were the mohalla dogs so they wouldn't intrude into the boundaries of his home.

Morning we lay awake, wondering what next, when Ramzana, took some boiling water and continued adding gur till his mother almost pulled away the gur-kanastar from his hands. Then his mother neared and asked us where we are going or coming from, and added that these were like the Partition times she had witnessed when even dying humans were not spared. She wanted us to leave her place almost immediately al-though Ramzana kept telling her that he's taking us to a Pandit's hotel for work. The mother looked angrily at him before throwing out, sentence after sentence—'Ramzana, you always been a duffer! Don't you know your Panditjee will be too scared to keep these Musalmaans. Not even if they clean his shit holes. His hotel will be set on fire. I'm certain even our "jhopra" will be destroyed by these goondas walking around and staring at these boys . . . they look Musalmaans and we Musalmaans!'

He'd let his mother go on and on, not even shutting her up when she dragged along his not-marrying and not producing a single child! All that he said in that rather subdued way, perhaps because the mohalla people don't get to hear, *'Bahut achha hua shaadi nahin kee. Dekh rahee ho musalmano ka kya haal ho raha hai . . . yeh bachchai bhaag rahein hain, bhukai-pyase hain.'*(Good I didn't marry. Can't you see what the Muslims are going through. These poor kids are running around, all too hungry and thirsty.)

Panditjee's hotel was not too close; in fact, far. At least that is what I felt or that is what it seemed, with our run down condition. Around noon we finally reached the other end of the road, where near a bus stand we stopped with a huge board dangling upside down—Out came a very old man with a gentle looking face to him. While we sat on the charpoy, Ramzana told him details to us and if we could be employed as cleaners or helpers. The smile faded from his face, instead worrying frowns took over. *'Nahin . . . nahin! Musalmaano ko nahin rakh sakte hain. Yahan ke sab customer bhaag jahein gai . . . waise bhi dhanda chaupat ho gaya hai, dangon ke baad sab khatam ho gaya hai.'* (No . . . No. Can't keep Muslims here. All our customers will run away. As it is business is all down and over after the communal rioting.)

We sat there lifeless, with the dishevelled-looking Ramzana looking more than upset. He threw glances at us and then at his cart—as though caught between the two. In between, he plucked a Neem branch and kept thrusting it all too enthusiastically all over his gums and teeth. Then once again walked towards that same man who'd minutes back refused to employ us. This time he was seen folding his hands and telling Ramzana to get going, gesturing towards the dhabas on the other side of the bus stand.

We somehow walked there; hunger weakening our limbs, so much so that we couldn't even speak out a full-fledged sentence. Nah, nothing beyond a couple of words. Two sardars (Sikh men) looked all too preoccupied, shoving rotis into a tandoor. One of them took out his bent head and asked Ramzana if he's got along his relatives for *khaana–peena* to the dhaba. The way Ramzana had looked at him relayed a bundle of sentiments—helplessness and sadness. He almost cried out—'*Lachaar agar hum nahin hotai to inn becharai bachon ko aapke tandoor se nikli hue rotiyan zaroor khilata . . . Lachaar hun.*' (I'm helpless, otherwise would have definitely made these children eat rotis made in your tandoor but right now I'm helpless.)

Before he could say a word more, that sardar man took out a charpoy and placed a steel plate with daal in a small bowl and several rotis spread out around the bowl. No, Ramzana didn't touch a morsel, instead spent the next five minutes, requesting him if we boys could be employed there. The man kept nodding, 'But only these two older ones. These boys will have sweep the floors and clean all the utensils here and in the kitchen above, where my family lives. Yes, they just arrived from Punjab.'

Imtiaz and I were left there. Ramzana carted back to his home, Sultan and Sohail. No, he couldn't peddle this time because of the boys' weight but kept dragging it along. No, not till about very far.

No sooner we had begun sweeping the sprawling courtyard and backyard to this dhaba, one of the boys, Sultan, came running towards us to say that Ramzana says that he will come along tomorrow to see whether we are okay otherwise he will take us all to another place. With brooms clutched in our hands we nodded, only to see more litter and dirt piled all around. Barely had we cleaned the floors came the turn of utensils; cleaning utensils in the dhaba and many more of them in the kitchen attached to the rooms upstairs. But as soon as the three women saw me cleaning the utensils they took to talking aloud before one of them asked me my name and where I came from. I forgot to add that Pahari prefix to my name. Instead said—Kashmiri. Their expressions changed and one of them started calling out to the menfolk down below, cursing them for keeping a Kashmiri right there on their heads!

For the next several minutes fierce arguments took off, with the men refusing to believe I was a Kashmiri but the women were insistent. And as they bombarded me with question after question, I told them that yes I'm a Kashmiri but no terrorist . . . been studying in a madrasa till shifted to another madrasa which was attacked and vandalized.

They came out with their verdict. No, no Kashmiri for them. Not because they were Muslim-bashers or Kashmiri-haters but the police would come knocking on the very front door to their dhaba.

They threw as many rotis as they could into two papery bags called lifafas, and told us to sit outside the dhaba. Wait for Ramzana or walk back to his home.

No, we couldn't have walked back on our own. And anyway as he had sent a message that he would come in the morning so thought we could spend the night on the cot. Kept seeing the men and women get off the buses, though for some reason not many passengers around. I sat comparing this bus stand with the Jammu bus stand and the comparison was startling. . .All too startled we sat up, as the women shouted from the first floor that we should immediately get moving from their compound as they didn't want any trouble from the police wallahs!

We walked towards bus stand, but there wasn't a single bench or even a boulder where we could sit. Walked still further and again nothing at all. No, not even street lights. We kept walking. At some distance lights flickered. And not too far a half closed or one could say half open shop shutter. Voices from within, as two or three men came out and another lot went inwards. They didn't bother to see us, at least they did not react seeing us. My stupid idea that we also peep into the half closed shutter—maybe, just maybe there's food and water in there. Barely had we walked somewhere near it, an hunched old man came out with a rounded bottle clutched in one of his hands and a gaudily done up woman clutched in the other hand, 'You two too young to be here, to be doing all this useless stuff. Get lost, out from here . . . from my sight!' Leaving all too suddenly, leaving back a trail of *itr*. (locally made perfume)

Should we still peep into that shutter?

No, said Imtiaz. He said he was sure that the place had all sorts of cheap people stuffed in there. No, he refused to talk or detail any further.

Like deadened creatures we two sat under the road side trees. Sitting all wide awake. And though a dozen or more rotis were there in those two lifafas duly clutched in our hands but gone was that desire to even touch a single roti.

No strays around—dogs or otherwise. Only around dawn a jeep halted not too far. The man driving the open jeep looked around. Before he started the jeep he threw ample glances at us. Then backed, after going ahead for a couple of minutes. He stood in front of us, looking at our faces before asking us what we doing there at dawn?

His look was so very focused that we blurted every single detail to our loitering around and before we knew what was happening or what could happen to us, he told us to sit in that jeep. Sit, sit, sit, he said all too impatiently.

Just too petrified to ask any questions, we sat in the jeep all too frightened. Awaiting with bated breath the what-next, till the jeep braked in front of Ramzana dwelling! He rushed out, followed by his mother, scowling at us or perhaps scowling seemed part of her gaze. That scowl on her face intensifying with a tinge of bitterness overtaking, when she saw Imtiaz and I huddled on that back seat. Somewhat un-moving our stares too, as Ramzana rather too spontaneously hugged the driver of the jeep, '*Zamindar sahib aapne yeh kya zahmat kee . . . hamarai gharib khane aane kee. Mujhe bulwa diya hota, mai hazir hota aapki khidmat mein.*' (Zamindar sahib, why did you take the trouble of coming to my dwelling. You should have sent a message and I would have come and met you.)

The man looked about in that strangely perturbed way before he said, '*Kaisai bulatai hum! Hamare sab log to yahaan se chalai gaie . . . sirf tum yee bachai ho.*' (How could I have called you? All my men have gone from here. Only you left here.) He stopped all too suddenly, and turned to look at us and then once again at Ramzana, '*Yeh bacche . . . inka yahan rahna theek nahin. Abhi apnee haveli ki taraf jaa raha hoon, inko bhi lae jaa raha hoon. Yahan mahaul theek nahin hai! Mai inn bachhon ko phir kuch rooz mein Lucknow lai jaonga.*' (Not okay for these children to be here. Conditions not okay. Just now I'm going towards my haveli and will take them along. And after some days will take them from my haveli to Lucknow.)

Looking distraught and exhausted, Sultan and Sohail also stood around, before being made to sit by our side. I could no longer sit still. I slumped, only to hear that man shriek, 'See they have begun to faint! *Dekho yeh baihosh ho rahe hain, yeh bacche burai haal mai hain.*' (See, they beginning to faint, all these kids in a bad condition.)

Without waiting for Ramzana's reaction, he kept saying, 'No wasting time. Taking them to my haveli. Starting off. Just now.'

He drove very fast, looking back, coming up with half-sentences more to himself than to the four of us. We continued hearing his hurried nervous outpourings: 'Haveli just here. Now nobody there but earlier it was full of people. My abba, ammi, apa all gone . . .resting in their graves. Now nobody there but I'm not leaving! But leaving you all soon, taking you all to Lucknow. Here no longer safe for us. Those creatures roaming around, looking for any excuse to provoke and then kill! Nah, not meat-eating, but these Sanghis can kill me, after accusing me of buying or selling beef! They eyeing my haveli, but I'm giving it to that new Trust for yateems and also for that new orphanage and that Centre for . . .'

He went on talking and talking of how life changed for him after the Hindutva brigades went about attacking. I can't remember all the gaalis (abuses) he had kept on and on muttering, as those were all in Hindi or Urdu. No, I'd never heard my parents ever abusing at home, not even when they looked angry and upset with the curfews and crackdowns and that constant news of killings.

My diary, will stop here as my eyes have begun watering. I hope my eyes are okay because they turning reddish, watering. Will write after resting my poor eyes.

5 November—4 a.m.

He didn't have to drive very far. After minutes, he braked. This time gently. Opening the door, 'Haveli . . . my haveli. Get in quickly!' He looked around, kept nodding as we stood outside the dilapidated structure called haveli.

Never had heard the word haveli in my life but thought it to be some big house, but here it was this crumbling place, with the boundary walls falling apart, bricks and more bricks lying around in heaps.

What haveli! I kept muttering as broken walls stood out and on one side a couple of rooms in some sort of a semi-broken down condition. Also, the ongoing barking of a dog tied rather too carelessly to the huge Neem tree standing tall, not too far from the broken walls.

I've been just too petrified of dogs right from the time I could crawl towards the front door of our Srinagar home. Father used to tell us that earlier when he was a kid he rarely saw stray dogs near our homes but now with security men around, eating and throwing food all over, these dogs thriving and moving about in packs. Each time he would bring up this topic, he would invariably end by saying he's read in our akhbars that it's the Israeli agencies strategy to unleash stray dogs in the midst of the Palestinian refugees so that hundreds are bitten and die of rabies. The same strategy the sarkari agencies of Hindustan are adopting in our Kashmir, on us Kashmiris!

And as soon as the man tried to untie the rope from the dog's collar, I shrieked and howled . . . uncontrolled my shrieks even as the man came up gently towards me, telling me that he will not untie the dog.

Though I had stopped crying but my yearning for home unstoppable. I longed to be back, to my home. Somehow I was missing Gulzar so much that I felt that I could no longer contain my pain. No, I didn't touch a morsel of the daal–rotis the man got from the next room. Till, the man brought a spoonful of that daal close to my lips. Gulzar used to do exactly that when I would refuse to eat, but instead of daal, it used to be our everyday food— boiled rice and haaq. I swallowed that spoonful of daal. For the first time that scowl on the man's seemed lessening and a sad smile overtaking.

Imtiaz, Sohail, and Sultan also looked somewhat less tense seeing me eat. Also to hear this man talk in that ongoing way. He telling us that he buys many rotis and some daal from the roadside dhabas. 'Earlier ammi supervised all the cooking in the bawarchi-khaana but that was many years ago. Now ammi, abba, and my sister buried in our qabristan. I'm also near dead, with everything going away from us. Now hardly one or two Muslim families left here. Many have left this place and the surrounding villages after the 2013 riots. Earlier we zamindars lived like nawab sahibs but all's gone!'

I don't know why, but I didn't have the nerves to hear all those details of the systematic ruin he was detailing. And in the midst of hearing him, the *roti-ka-niwalaa* (a small piece of the roti – a morsel) got stuck in my throat and had to vomit it out, with this man thumping my back, with me left muttering 'I'm not getting used to roti . . . we Kashmiris used to having our boiled rice.' Somehow I couldn't hold back my Kashmiri identity, even as Imtiaz kept pressing my foot—for me to shut up! But then it was late . . . too late! Though I was anticipating this man to be getting up all too charged or super charged hearing the word 'Kashmiri' but he looked happy! Yes, he actually looked happy. His face lit up!

He asked me to repeat. He kept on saying repeatedly in that childlike way. 'Tell me again you a Kashmiri! You Kashmiri but you not too fair! Maybe this heat here ruined your looks.'

Imtiaz rather too nervously kept dipping rotis, one after another, in the daal while the other two boys stuffed their mouth with mouthfuls of the *daal-roti niwalaas*, but here was I looking at this man who was also staring at my face in a strangely affectionate way. Bonding of a definite sort.

It was for the very first time in all these months, after I was transported far away from my home to Dilli and then further down to this region, that I'd met a person who looked so very happy knowing that I am a Kashmiri. Otherwise either I was made to look self-conscious or forced to getting apologetic. To the extent of introducing myself as a Pahari or what!

Before I could gather the confidence to ask whether he knows anyone in Kashmir, the barks of the dog overtook, breaking free the dog rushed towards us. Though this man caught him in time but this time my crying wouldn't stop and I started blabbering in Kashmiri.

Imtiaz and the other boys tried consoling me. I kept pleading, I wanted to get back home, to my Srinagar. He looked about helplessly and asked me to give him my father's mobile number so that he could make me talk to him and then decide what to do. I was amazed, I remembered all the digits, rattled off the number. And though he tried many, many times but at first the ring wouldn't go through and then some sort of ongoing ringing of the bell. 'Seems no mobile connectivity there . . . what else. So many times trying but not connecting.' He kept trying. Not giving up. Asking me if I knew or remembered any other number.

None.

Then what? How do I go back to my Srinagar?

The more he asked me, rather re-asked me to try recollecting any other mobile number, I grew impatient. Strangely he didn't look angry; on the contrary saying rather too calmly, 'Earlier I knew several Kashmiris but not now. Tell me how to send you back?'

You know Kashmiris?

'Knew a shawl seller and his family; he used to get his family to Muzaffarnagar every winter. I'd even visited Srinagar on their invitation but that was years back. Now no idea where they!'

This middle-aged man was talking to us as though he our long lost friend. Rattled, we didn't know how to react to his offloading. All these months it was only the maulvis talking in that matter of fact way and that too about gunah-sawaab and also about Dozakh-Jannat. It's for the first time that a man was talking to us like a friend. We didn't have to ask him a thing because before we could, he was himself telling us one thing after another. As though it's after months he had found a small assembly of listeners, he went on and on, 'Let me see in one of the papers kept on the shelf whether those Kashmir telephone numbers are there. Maybe scribbled in one of those papers . . . just maybe. Actually after my abba died of Alzheimer's I feel what's there to remember when one fine day one can sit there forgetting everything. I have anyway tried my best to forget everything about Kashmir because I couldn't get to marry Firdous. You boys too young to understand what I'm saying. My mother was too old to understand about my feelings; she didn't bother to give a damn about my emotional feelings. She always kept saying how can a zamindar's son marry a shawl seller's sister! That was the end of my love! Really loved Firdous . . . too many memories. I didn't even keep one shawl with me . . . distributed all to the mohalla people but see the same mohalla people torched my haveli during the dangas. Ammi kept begging them to spare our haveli but who was there to listen, to see how those saala goondas were hounding us. Ammi collapsed seeing them firing, killing my sister. Now nobody left in my clan! If I go, those goondas will take over. Sticking around but not sure till when. What for! Nobody left in my life! Got to know from other shawl sellers, my Firdous married off to someone in Doda. I'm not marrying. You boys too young to know what pain is all about!'

I couldn't really understand why he couldn't get to marry Firdous and why did he have to distribute all the shawls he had with him—if he still had them with him, he could have easily given us as there was a certain definite chill in the air. Must say his talks different—refreshingly different from the maulvis typical sermons along the dos and don'ts strain.

We lay down exhausted on a sprawling takht and though the dog had continued barking but there wasn't an uff from us!

9 November—6 a.m.

Yesterday early morning I saw Ramzana drag his cart towards the Neem tree and then sit under it, looking all too forlorn and upset. This person, 'zamindar sahib', though he insists we call him Musarrat mia, was also up and about. And though he was about to walk out but then sat down on the broken side boundary wall when Ramzana told him loud and clear that 'the village people were asking about these four boys here. Want to know so much about them. Will be safe if you shift them out from here. Your weapons are also all taken away by the sarkar, so what happens when those goonda creatures attack your haveli. It's their sarkar they can do anything! They'll know these are Musalmaan boys so you know what could happen!'

This man's face turned pale and so did mine. I woke up the other boys and told them exactly all this. So the calm in our lives was so very short lived!

Though I neared the broken wall, to get to hear what he plans to do with our lives or with us but didn't get to hear a single word. This man quietly getting up and putting a pan full of water on the gas. For some strange reason he was nodding to himself even while adding sugar and milk to the water and then stopped all too suddenly, and quietly went up to Ramzana, 'Chacha, stop. Just stop. Can't hear these details. These boys anyway look so very frightened and that Kashmiri boy been crying. Will take them out from here to some safe place!'

All that Ramzana could barely squeak, 'Kashmiri . . . who Kashmiri here! That thanedar sahib's orders to inform him if any Kashmiri is to be spotted here.' Before he could say a word more, rather before a single word could come out of his mouth, this zamindar man, Musarrat mia, put his hand on Ramzana's mouth and with the other hand put a knife across his neck. 'Know all my hathiyars (weapons) are with those police wallahs but not these chakoos and churees (knives). Will do your jhatka or halaal right here. Get going and don't you dare tell a word of this even to your amma. Don't trust her one bit, sits all day with the sarpanch's sisters. Don't you and your mother know that sarpanch been eyeing my haveli. Will burn this place but not give him an inch from here!'

Ramzana sat there unmoving. Not even as this zamindar gave him that brew in a glass and poured out the remains of it in four mugs and then sat back, with the mobile clutched close to his chest. Seeing Ramzana unmoving he took out some terrible gaalis—saala harami . . . haramzada! Making the cart-puller pull along his cart at some maddening speed.

Seeing me standing there he didn't really look very surprised but rather too gently told me to get going inwards and lock the door as he had to unleash the dog. Then added, 'Are you all up? We got to get moving from here . . . we going far away from here but you'll be safe. Now let me open the dog for some time before we leave. Boys take chai inwards. There's nothing to eat, maybe one or two rotis are left in the Naimat Khaanaa (cupboard with front jaali for adequate ventilation, to keep food, fruit and other eatables). Earlier when ammi was alive it used to be full of food but nothing in there. See, maybe some papey.' (locally made biscuits).

Naimat Khaanaa! Never before had heard this word. It sounded so very good. And so very okay with food. Food is Naimat! Ask me!

Imtiaz and the other two boys were awake. Imtiaz told me that he wants to get back to his place which couldn't be very far from here. No, he did not want to be transported any further and was all set to ask Musarrat mia to put him on a bus. He asked me if I would also like to come along. And I don't know why he kept repeatedly saying, ' Will die in my home only, not here or there . . . no one of my qasbah can kill me in my home, they all know what my abba's plants have done to settle their boils and blood pressure and what other pressures!'

I unbolted the door as the dog's bark lessened. Saw Musarrat mia feeding the dog what seemed like rotis soaked in watery milky concoction.

I hurriedly got back, inside the room, where Imtiaz once again tried convincing me, 'Gull, see sense. Please come with me to my home. Will tell everyone you from the hills. Will tell them that your people also into plants.' Seeing me look unconvinced, he furthered, 'Come with me; you also wanted to collect Mehndi leaves for your ammi and nani. Lots and lots of shrubs there in my orchards and baghs and gardens . . . all free for you. Will let you pluck as many flowers and leaves as you want to. And you can even sell them when you get back to your Kashmir. Our leaves and flowers can treat any disease. We can do all this business together.'

Before he could say more, Musarrat mia, was there knocking, telling us that the dog is tied back and we start off immediately.

But when Imtiaz told him that he is taking me to his place and the other two boys can also come along with us, he lost his cool. He asked Imtiaz to repeat the name of the place and with that he looked and sounded explosive, 'So many Muslim families moved from there! All rushing to Dilli to work as mazdoors. All zamindars of those yesteryears are now doing mazdoori in Dilli or sitting under those tattered tents. Know all running away from there, told them to come here but even here halaats too bad. I can drop you off on the highway or wherever you want to go, but wouldn't let you ruin the lives of these three. This Kashmiri will be killed the minute he is to be spotted there.'

But Imtiaz was more than adamant.

We sat in the jeep.

Before we could gather the courage or the confidence to ask where we were heading, he came up with quick sentences, 'Driving to Lucknow and will leave you there at a place where Islamic teaching and other studies given to children. It's safe and you will get some food too. Imtiaz can decide whether his plants and trees are more important than his life. His village or qasbah is on the way, along that bypass.'

I looked at Imtiaz, as he kept shaking his head in that obstinate way, 'Will go to my lands, my trees, my plants . . . will go to my home. Let me be there. My ammi's qabr also there, have to go for fateha. Home is home.'

9 November—very late night—scribbling away, writing as much as I can. Don't know the time, not even keeping track of the time passing by.

Musarrat mia was concentrating less on his driving, looking less towards the road and more backwards, focusing on the mutterings coming from the back seat. Though initially he didn't react but then did. He tried to explain to Imtiaz that the people of his area are no longer what they used to be, as political goons and land mafia have made inroads, polluting their innocent minds, ruining the very place and the people living on that stretch of land.

But within the next several minutes when Imtiaz's mutterings turned into a full-fledged demand, Musarrat mia, assured him that he would be driving along the bypass, leading inwards, towards his place.

In the next 40 or 50 minutes, we were at the bypass, but it seemed blocked by huge tree branches spread out, as though flung around to block all outside movement. Like a child possessed, Imtiaz shrieked, 'My trees! All my trees cut and chopped!' No, he brushed aside any reasoning to suggest that those logs could be cut off from any tree and not from the ones growing in his orchards and lands. But he was un-moved, from his sheer determination or obsession to call them his very own trees! He kept muttering—his leaves, fruit, twigs, and whatever else was there to those lofty branches!

I don't know how to describe, but he was inconsolable and when Musarrat mia suggested to him that he will have to jump over those branches as the jeep tyres could get stuck, he'd looked somewhat scared or nervous and kept saying his home was another two kilometres away. So the vehicle went over the branches and logs, but then several men came from the adjacent fields with huge lathis in their hands. Musarrat mia drove on . . . there was little choice or no other option because to reverse would mean to face the enemy right there.

He kept on driving, with Imtiaz giving those directions to the various inroads. Finally the inroad leading to his home. The kothi standing out, surrounded by trees and more trees. Yes, quite like he'd described to me over a hundred times. How the trees surrounded his home. It was all too offbeat.

Musarrat mia looked tense but decided to leave him till the entrance to the kothi. We followed only to see it flooded with people. From Imtiaz's expressions, it was more than obvious he didn't recognize even one of them and when he looked about angrily, those men neared and asked him to get out. When he cried out that it's his home they got terribly aggressive, 'All that in the past, we the new owners! Musalmaans out . . . now our home . . . out you creatures!'

Don't know how to describe the terrorized look on Imtiaz's face. He cried out but those men smirked, one of them even threatened to kill him. But Imtiaz was till adamant, unmoving from there, as though he was hell bent on getting killed in his home but we dragged him back to the vehicle. Barely had we crossed over to the next inroad, those men with lathis rushed towards our vehicle from the front and side and some even from the back. Shouting hysterically, 'Don't let these Musalmaans get going. Kill. Just kill! All looking Musalmaans. All to be killed by us, here and right now!'

Though Musarrat mia continued driving even in the circumstances, the moment he loosened or lessened his grasp on Imtiaz's arm, the boy jumped out of the vehicle!

In the next couple of seconds all that we could see was Imtiaz surrounded by those wolf looking men, shrieking all sorts of slogans. In between came his cries and then all those cries ebbed with Jai Shri Ram slogans overtaking the entire expanse.

Musarrat mia continued driving. Don't ask me at what speed but drove like a man possessed. Braking only in front of a police thana. Without saying a word to us, he rushed inwards. We sat on the verge of a breakdown. Several police men came out with him but I couldn't see even one of the three parked police vehicles taking off. Sitting back on the driver's seat, Musarrat mia kept dialling and re-dialling many mobile numbers, telling them of the lynching of Imtiaz.

No, no sign of urgency from the police. Finally two constables on bikes told us to direct them to the site. And even when we told them there were over two dozen men armed with lathis and weapons and what not, the cops showed little urgency.

Musarrat mia kept on driving, the two cops following us. When we reached the site where Imtiaz was first dragged to, we could see his semi-clad body tied to an electric pole.

No sign of the killers, not one from the lynch brigade, to be seen around. Musarrat braked, told the two cops to follow him to Imtiaz's home, occupied by the goondas and killers, but the two cops looked unsure and then one of them insisted that they would first have to take the body for post mortem. No, no urgency in arresting his killers!

One car stopped. Musarrat's two friends—Arun and Afsar—whom he had called. And as these two men tried to tell the cops to arrest the killers of Imtiaz, they were threatened to get going otherwise they would be arrested for the lynching of Imtiaz!

Musarrat mia was left with no other option but to follow the cops' orders. We drove back to the police station carrying Imtiaz battered frame.

And while Musarrat and the cops carried Imtiaz's battered frame to some hospital for post mortem we were made to sit in the friends' car to be driven to Bareilly.

The three of us sat back, while two men drove, taking turns. Throughout they kept talking of the communal violence spreading out, severely affecting the Musalmaans of the country. I couldn't really give a damn whether we were getting driven towards hell or heaven or wherever! Anger was building up within me—I don't know why father sent me here!

Why so many Muslims running about for safety, killed in this place. Why was Imtiaz lynched! Just because he was a Muslim orphan boy trying to go back to his home and lands and gardens. Why do I have to go all over trying to hide the fact that I'm a Kashmiri Muslim. Why all the stupid lies that I'm a Pahari! Why should I be made to feel so scared . . . so scared!

I wanted to open the car door and get running back to my Srinagar but then sat back, knowing that my Srinagar is miles away and I could be lynched a hundred times on the way!

One of the men turned to see whether we were awake or if we had dozed off. They halted the car near some eatery and though we didn't ask for a thing but they got along three biscuit packets and one big bottle of water. I didn't want to touch a single biscuit and kept them on the side. The same man who saw me putting the biscuit packets aside slowly opened all three packets, 'Bareilly is far . . . don't know whether we get food at home. Nobody knows I'm carrying guests. Eat. These biscuits good ones.' The other man who looked much too exhausted with the driving, added, 'You want to have anything else to eat? Nothing to worry. Consider me to be your uncle. Call me Arun chacha.'

The two boys, Sohail and Sultan, nudged me and re-nudged. When I didn't react, they whispered in my ear, 'He some Hindu . . . don't know whether we'll be left alive!'

Though startled, after seeing Imtiaz killed, I couldn't be bothered whether the two men driving us were Hindus or Muslims, whether they were taking us ahead to cut and chop our bodies or be throwing us into a furnace!

They braked as the traffic piled up at a rail phatak and then got out and walked about. The second they went out of the car, we three offloaded severe apprehensions—May be we get sold off! Maybe we would be also lynched! Maybe our flesh cut into bits and pieces and thrown about!

Now they have stopped at some roadside motel or hotel. I'm writing sitting in this car. What else to do. Let me write till they are back.

Maybe they take hours to get back as they saying they too tired to drive any further. Sohail and Sultan look very upset, more so as we aren't even sure where we are heading.

They are talking non-stop about Imtiaz.

Before I could write some more, they got back, with a packet full of apples and one of them—Arun—gave us an apple each, along with that telling us that he had managed to speak to Musarrat mia and post mortem done and now they would be preparing for the boy's burial there. Though he slowly added that till now the police hadn't arrested even one of the killers. The other man, Afsar, took over, *'Yeh police log sab jaantai hain. Kisi mantri ya uske santri ka phone aa gaya hoga.'* (these police men know everything. Some minister or his aide must have called them.)

We were too petrified to even utter a word. But the remaining way to Bareilly was enough to know what was going on in the state, as these two men spoke and spoke out of the ground realities. Both speaking among themselves; those to and fro of words between the two kept them all too charged.

You know, till now I'd only met and interacted and lived with Muslims. Now, for the very first time in my life I was hearing a Hindu speak out. And Arun spoke out about Dalits and Muslims getting completely side lined not only in Uttar Pradesh and all over the country.

All through the way, if one of them would give a longish description of a Dalit flogged to death by Hindutva goons, the other would go ahead and come up with an equally horrifying description of a Muslim lynched to death by Right-Wing brigades. And after that, both would say, 'Enemy the same . . . dushman same. Same lot killing us. Making us sit so very worried and apprehensive, just too unsure of our everyday existence!'

It seemed the two suddenly realized that we were sitting so very petrified after seeing our friend Imtiaz so very brutally attacked and killed, so some distractions thrown our way, 'Bareilly very close . . . only some miles away. We go home and you sleep. Very safe at my place. Our Dalit basti safest for you. None of these Sanghis can enter our basti, so you madrasa boys can stay in our homes. When Musarrat was in big trouble during the 2013 dangas and all ruined for him, we forced him to come to stay in my basti. We know him for many years. Today all such khandaani persons getting ruined here. Mafia looting their lands and homes.'

Before he could turn towards the main road, Afsar's mobile rang in that persistent way. And as he'd kept saying, 'Jee haan. . . Jee bilkul.' (Yes . . .and yes) a dozen times rather too nervously in quick succession, thought another emergency could well be on way. Not really. As he turned to tell us, 'We had to first go to Arun's home. Now Musarrat also reaching Bareilly. We all going to my place and then from there we going straight towards Lucknow. My house very big and many of my relatives

also stay around, so none of the Sanghis can dare near the front gates.'
But while he was telling us all this in a rather high-pitched voice, Arun's
mobile also rang in that persistent way and he too was talking rather too
nervously, and then all too suddenly almost yelling at Afsar to drive as
fast as he possibly could. His words still ringing in my ears, '*Nahin yaar,
tumhare yaa hamare ghar nahin. Sanghis ghoom rahen hain. Mantriyon
ke goonde* bhi *hamare peechaa kar rahen hain.*' (Not your home and nor
mine. Hindutva lot roaming around. And the minister's men also following us.)

For what seemed to me endless minutes the two men had continued
arguing—where to take the three of us. They seemed ruling out place after
place, vetoing each other's suggestions, countering their own arguments
with what they called pros and cons. It baffled me that they were even
considering taking us for safe refuge to a mandir and then also coming up
was the mention of a gurudwara and then a church and also names of two
or three masjids.

We looked at each other, more than nervous. I didn't realize that
Imtiaz's killers would be so very blood thirsty, so much so that entire
Hindutva brigades would be following us. The car halted all too suddenly,
as Afsar threw up his hands, exclaimed that he was just too exhausted!

Just then Arun exclaimed that he knows where it would be the safest
for us. And he asked Afsar to shift from the driver's seat. Behind the wheel
and looking more than confident he drove at some maddening speed.
Braking only when the car almost rammed into a row of graves!

Afsar screamed, 'What! Getting us to a qabristan! What's wrong ...
what's happening!'

I looked more than at ease, for in my Srinagar I have seen graves after
graves. Gulzar and I have played around graves. As father used to tell us
that the dead are not really dead but merely resting in their graves!

While the two men were talking to a grave digger standing not too far
from one of the graves in this qabristan, I sat around hopelessly, much
too exhausted. Didn't react or perhaps I didn't even want to react when
I heard Arun telling that grave digger that as of now there's no dead form
around but if those Hindutva brigades follow us, trace us here, then
maybe all of us will need the earth to wrap up our frames! 'Yes, even mine.
Though I'm Hindu but let me be also buried with my Muslim friends.
After all, so many Hindus also lie buried not only in those years gone by,

but even now. Wasn't Jayalalitha buried! And other Madrasi Dravidians also buried in that Marina beach in Chennai.'

The grave digger looked dazed to see so many alive sit close to the graves and that too without an uff! He kept looking dazed, 'Bhaiyya I can't understand. Why you all here! Tell me, just let me know where's the maiyyat ... where's the dead body? Is the dead being brought here? Tell me so that I start off digging the grave. Why waste my time and yours too. Tell me, is the dead a child or a zenana or a mardana or a hijra or a tawaif so that I dig the grave accordingly?'

Arun got up and told him rather too blatantly that we are trying to hide from goondas, who have lynched a boy and now are trying to chase us, to kill us, because we reported to the police. Not that the police will do a thing to them as those murderers are no ordinary murderers, but part of some Hindutva brigade!

That grave digger looked as though he himself would lie dead, '*Hai Daiyya*! *Yeh Zulm*! *Zalim sarkar.*' (What! What anarchy, what a wicked sarkar)

He then sat with us, ever so subdued; after a definite lull, pointing towards a freshly dug grave, sighing while saying in a matter of fact way, 'Only an hour back buried one young *bitiya* (girl). All those coming with the *maiyya*t saying that she wanted to marry some Shia bhaiyya of her chowk mohalla but her abba–ammi locked her up. She gave up her life . . . dead . . . khatam! Now her people crying and sobbing but now what's left. She gone! See her grave! Her freshly made resting place!'

As the night peaked, this grave digger came up with more and more details to the dead he'd been burying for years, which included his baby son too. 'Now nobody with me . . . my biwi went mad and took her all over for ilaaj—first to Dewa Sharif and then to Noor Manzil and then Ajmer Sharif but nothing getting okay with her. Sorrow turned her completely mad and insane. She started walking all around these graves searching for my son Saleem's grave. Like you people she also coming here at night . . . daytime women are not allowed here so whilst I used to go to sleep she used to slip off and be here, going from qabr to qabr. Too much for me, so sent her off to her village. There they are tying her legs because there also she roaming around the village, going from one qabr to the next.'

We sat there till about dawn when this grave digger told us that it wouldn't be safe we are seen sitting here as several mohalla persons come here to pray. Fateha at the graves.

Where do we go? asked Arun. With Afsar telling that grave digger that we would need to be here till noon as another of their friends would be reaching here and by then they'd have decided whether they would go further or stay put in Bareilly.

The grave digger shook his head. 'Not safe . . . not safe . . . even our qabristan is under watch. Built on wafq land, it is being eyed by that wafq minister, Naqash Naqvi. He coming here from Lucknow every second or third day. What if he sees you all here and your car . . . surely he'll ask all sorts of questions. Who's there to answer all those questions but me! Manager sahib is very unwell, after all, he is got dengue and the other grave digger, Raheem, in Dilli, for his nikah so only I'm here to answer all sorts of questions of these sarkari saalas. Hearing them talk of building some big bazaar here. Don't they know that even the dead can curse but they not bothered!'

Seeing us get up in that hopeless way he came up with an idea: 'If you people have no other place to go, then my hut is at the other end other of the qabristan but leave the car far away because not many Musalmaans have cars today so immediately whoever comes here will ask—whose car and then all other details will automatically come out. And then my grave will also be dug here!'

We walked in that strangely sapped way—a combination of a strange sort of fatigue cum tension, compounded by this strange way of trying to hide, in the strangest of hideouts.

We followed him, entered his hut—with a nothingness to it hanging about in great abundance! Nothing in there except for a cot and a gas stove and pile of utensils and a plastic container brimming with water or water look alike as it looked greyish coloured water. Till now I was under the impression that the madrasas where I had stayed were ill equipped— that is nothing beyond the basics—but after seeing and sitting in this grave digger's hut, I realized that this was actually equipped with a nothingness to it! He offered us nothing—there was nothing to be offered!

Arun and Afsar kept dialling and re-dialling numbers and finally managed to get through to Musarrat mia. Though they didn't tell us any of the details except that he is coming here and he will be taking us to Lucknow.

They looked not just very tired but as though they couldn't take any more of the strain of trying to save us from getting lynched.

It was only around noon that the grave digger came running in to tell that a car had stopped beyond the broken boundary wall and two men were seen coming this side.

Two men! Exclaimed Arun and Afsar but Musarrat mia had to come alone here. Then sat back looking relaxed when the grave digger added that one of the men looked a sardar sahib. Arun and Afsar smiled, 'Must be Balli bhai . . . now all okay. Balli is there then all okay. Musarrat must have left his jeep there, and got here in Balli's car. Sensible. Not safe to be driving all alone in this sort of situation!'

Musarrat mia seemed to have aged ten years in these hours. Hunched and pale faced he sat on the charpoy recounting his struggles to have the FIR lodged—the entire thana was besieged by the goondas of the area, shouting slogans, threatening to kill him. He said he left his vehicle there and had to call Balli to come with his factory men and then they forced the police to lodge the FIR. He kept saying he's certain that nothing will happen to that FIR. Looking very upset, repeating over and over again, 'The way they killed that child Imtiaz! Taubah, Taubah! Nobody seems safe . . . don't know what happens next . . . in my own country we fleeing like refugees. Don't want to be hounded, like this sarkar is hounding the Rohingyas as though they aren't humans, but animals. Sarkar not giving refuge to any one! Not even to their own people. Me and you!'

Though I wanted to tell them how sufis lying buried in my Kashmir were once upon a time refugees, I didn't want to. Futile, useless to open my mouth, but, yes, simply amazing. In those centuries past by how those sufis who had come fleeing from Central Asia had found not just refuge in my Kashmir but also got so much love from the locals. Toth used to tell us so many qissas to the sufis who'd fled from Central Asia, Iran and Iraq, coming to our Kashmir. And you know what, all our Kashmiris not only accepted them but became close to them. To this day their graves and dargahs stand in my Kashmir.

Writing from the grave digger's hut. Not sure of the time. No watch on us. Can't ask anyone. And as the hut is surrounded by trees so no sun rays.

Balli left almost immediately, saying his factory workers could be waiting for him. Musarrat mia looked exhausted. Said he needs some time. Finally, after an hour or so, when he did decide that we should all be moving out, the grave digger came running inwards, panting and patting his bald head 'Ghazab! *Ghazab ho gaya* . . . that mantri sahib here. Told you all he's here every second day. Driving all that way from Lucknow because his two eyes on this wafq land. A Musalmaan, but he is very terrible. Too greedy. He's coming here with all maps and designs with him. Telling you all, all the engineer sahibs with him, he wants many shops to be built here. He planning to crush all the bones and skeletons lying buried in these five hundred graves. What to hide from you all, had heard him tell the engineers that pull out all the dead and fling them out; he telling that after all what good are the dead.'

We sat back, staring at each other's tense faces, waiting for the grave digger to come again to tell us that the sarkari lot has departed so that we could also get moving from here.

Two or three hours passed by, but no sign of the digger and no other news. Except that Musarrat mia was constantly on his mobile—talking very softly and in that cautious way. All that he would mutter to us after every call, 'Once we reach Lucknow, this scare will not be there. Will keep you all in a safe place, away from this madness spreading out. Don't think too much about Imtiaz. He's resting in heaven, not like us zinda in this hell . . . hell here!'

For some strange reason or not really, all this Jannat-Dozakh muttering and utterings of Musarrat mia reminded me all too suddenly of my grandmother as she'd so very often quipped—how the rulers of the day have turned our Kashmir hellish, turned our Jannat into Dozakh!

Suddenly, rather too spontaneously I looked at Musarrat mia clutching his mobile . . . talking away. He realized that I'd been staring at the mobile. And no sooner he ended that call, he asked me, once again for my toth's number. I could hear the ring tone and that's about it. He tried twice or thrice but then the other two men threw up their hands together with words—'*Kashmir ka bura haal . . . nothing working there . . . sab thap hai! Mobile thap hain wahan! Khatam.*' (bad conditions in Kashmir. Nothing seems functioning there. Mobile connectivity down and out.)

I didn't realize tears were flowing out in that un-stoppable way . . . spreading out, on my cheeks. They all looked towards me, and instead of talking of our fleeing towards Lucknow or the post mortem findings conducted on Imtiaz lynched body or how long we'd to sit in the grave digger's dwelling, Arun tried to bring about a distraction of sorts—he tried talking of the Amarnath yatra and how he had taken his parents up there to the Shrine in the gupha cave and how the local Kashmiris had really helped. Stretching on the distraction by telling us about Pahalgam, the Lidder river flowing along, pebbles he had picked by its side, which still remain displayed in his drawing room. It looked as though he had transported himself there. His get-away short lived, as within the next two minutes, the grave digger, Kalloo Khan, arrived, looking devastated, 'You people don't understand! Why did you come here for all your hiding! This place only for the dead or the dying like me! Qayamat hai, mantri not moving from here! Ordered biryani and all sorts of food items from some big place! He meeting all possible people here, in this Bareilly qabristan! Can you people believe he holding a meeting right here!'

Nobody seemed to react. Too exhausted to even utter a word. Arun had the sense to pull out two hundred rupee notes from his trouser pocket and place them on Kalloo's palm—'get some food for us before we all die here and you have to fling our bodies into some grave and drag mine to some shamshan ghat.' Though Kalloo didn't return the notes but he kept shaking his head like a rusted pendulum, kept describing how many cars are parked right till the very entrance to this graveyard. He repeating, 'Wouldn't they ask so much khaana–peena for whom . . . for whom! What if their santris come right here to see who all eating rotis and botis! What if they check those botis cut from bakris or murgaas or bhaisaas or what!'

Musarrat Mia lost his cool, 'Go tell them that ten persons have to be buried here. Don't you eat something! Don't you bloody chew anything! Don't you buy anything to bloody gulp down! Go and get rotis and daal from the nearest dhaba. No gosht at all, otherwise these fellows will tear open all your lifafas to see whether it is gaiyya's or maiyya's or what!'

Kalloo went scurrying out. Like deadened or dying human forms we sat there awaiting, till Arun decided that he would have to step out to see what's been happening in the world outside this dwelling. And in the next couple of minutes, as he returned we realized that something or everything was over—at least on our food and the connected survival front! He was panting. He telling us in that breathless way that the same police lot, we met at that thana, where Imtiaz's dead fractured form was taken, were now to be seen standing around that minister. They were telling the minister that they were searching for those men—that is we all—who'd dared to fight for the FIR to be lodged against that lynching. The killers were some minister's khaas men—from his constituency! This thanedar looking for us! Even coming till this dead place! It's better if we had hidden at the shamshan ghat! One FIR and this hounding!'

What! I were feeling so weak as though wouldn't be able to see another day. And while writing, I had even peeped out of the twisted door to this dwelling, wondering where our qabrs would be get dug if I we die right here, at the graveyard or inside this dwelling. Another very, very upsetting thought hit—why on earth will this ageing grave digger Kalloo take the trouble of digging separate graves for each one of us, when he could dump us all in one big grave like they were doing in Kashmir. In my Kashmir, they call these mass graves. No, my father or my mother hadn't uttered a word on this to us, but I'd read it myself in the Urdu akhbars, that many, many dead bodies are getting stuffed in what they called mass graves. Remembering all those details I'd read in the akhbars, in maulvi sahib's room at one end of the dargah when father had sent two books for him. He was saying his nimaz, so whilst waiting for him, I began reading all the akhbars kept there. One even carrying all the details to the mass graves—one woman from America, some Chatterjee—yes, yes, Angana Chatterjee—had even done some research on the hundreds of our mass graves. She been asking whose graves? Who all are so very secretly buried, their dead forms dumped in mass graves?

Not sure whether mass graves are found to be here, in Uttar Pradesh's Bareilly. Maybe our mass grave here in Bareilly will be the first.

Didn't realize that Musarrat mia was also thinking of qabrs because before getting up all too impatiently he near shrieked, 'Don't like to be buried here but why will these Kalloos Salloos even be taking the trouble of burying us. Why will they be making us rest in peace! They will throw away our bodies here and there so that stray dogs pull away our bones. Have to get out from here!'

The two other men pulled him right back—The two words—daroga and thanedar seemed to make the zamindar sit back on charpoy!

He didn't have to sit back for too long as the grave digger arrived with the news that all the men have left. Their driver log discussing among themselves that they leaving towards Lucknow, taking the big sahibs to Lucknow for some big meeting. Police wallahs also left in that big jeep and two or three other motorcycles. So he could then get some khaana.

The rotis and daal he got along were such that if it was in my Kashmir I am certain that nobody could have touched them but here we all pounced on the rotis, tearing them, before dipping them in that plastic bowl full of daal which he insisted on placing it in the centre, engulfed by the pile of rotis. In the midst of fulfilling those hunger pangs I couldn't have counted their exact numbers but they were so many that they tumbling over. Then not so, as within minutes they were tucked right inside our tummies. For some strange reason the grave digger didn't tuck in a morsel, telling us that he has got to dig two graves right now, as two more dead bodies are on way from the old city.

He told us to wait inside the dwelling for another couple of hours but Musarrat mia and his two friends were in no mood to listen to any of the digger's logic—words along the strain that police wallahs could as well be standing at the crossing or simply driving all along the city or their khabariyas (informers) be parked at the highway. Then what!

I had heard in my Kashmir, men being lured and bought over by the Agencies to pass on information or to carry information or to spread around rumours. Once or twice I'd even overheard father telling mother about even school students getting used by the Agency people, they corrupting young girls too. Don't know what all he meant by all that.

Even as Musarrat mia tried to brush aside the grave digger's warnings and forewarning, he came up with a shocker of sorts—'*Sahib log mera kahna sunai, mai bhi pehle khabariya tha!*' (Listen to me, to what I'm saying, as earlier I'd worked as an informer.)

Though he'd tried to assure us that that was his past but Musarrat mia kept on muttering—once a khabariya, always a khabariya!

The dilemma continued even as Arun and Afsar glared at Kalloo. Quite obviously beyond that they couldn't do a thing. The ongoing suspense somewhat suspended by Musarrat mia asking him rather too blatantly if he had informed the minister and the police wallahs—about our whereabouts or about our further plans of driving towards Lucknow. The grave digger looked about angrily, as though almost accusing us of being a bunch of idiots. 'If I told them about you all here they could have killed you and your friends and even these boys! Encounters going on so much here. I too could have been killed! For informing them too late! Now you people be here for another hour or so and only then think of moving from here. I'm going to dig two more graves . . . don't know when the hell will I get to rest in my grave!'

Writing . . . sitting in the car, as we driving away from the graveyard.

The second Kalloo could be seen turning towards the broken edge to the graveyard, Arun and Afsar almost clung to each other in exasperation or what! With Musarrat mia's voice coming through loud and clear, 'Can't trust this Kalloo fellow. He could as well be changing his mind and telling them about us. Get going from here, immediately. No, not towards Lucknow but in the opposite direction.'

Though we could see Kalloo digging wholeheartedly, quite obviously we didn't want to stop by to tell him about our departure. He looked in our direction as Arun's car picked up speed. He even tried to open his mouth and raise his hands but then turned back seeing the car heading out.

I can't try describe the level of stress. If my father and mother had seen me like this, they would have collapsed. Even if they would see me sitting gloomy in our Srinagar home, they would ask a thousand questions, trying to probe what had upset me so much. Here I was living in a state where I was seeing death right there, hovering around me.

Toth used to tell us that no matter what we try or how hard we try, there is a time and place for everything or anything to happen or not happen!

When the car took another hurried turn, Afsar screamed he wanted to get out right there, almost getting hysterical that his home and children and wife are all stationed in Bareilly, so why should he be taking all this journey. But with Musarrat mia and Arun telling him of the cops looking out for us, the only option is not to be seen by them.

Nobody spoke a word as Arun continued driving. I could see the agricultural lands give way to semi-forested stretches and then glimpses of the mountainous range. Musarrat finally spoke, that from Bareilly we going upwards. He knows of Balli's sister's kothi in Kathgodam on the foothills.

Hills and mountains. My thoughts rather too automatically went back home, to my Kashmir Valley. And what beautiful mighty mountains stand out. Didn't realize their beauty till the day we had gone up to the Chashme Shahi springs and then that one school picnic at the resort near Gulmarg and that last outing with my mother and grandmother.

All I asked, more to ease the ongoing tension, whether herbs and fruit trees are growing on these mountains, where we were heading. I think I asked all this more because Imtiaz's memory was very much hovering around me—but the second I asked this—Musarrat snapped and told me to shut up! All along I had been marvelling his cool because except for making strange faces and muttering non-stop he hadn't screamed and shouted at us. But then now he did. Yelling, 'Risking my life but here you asking all this rubbish—herbs and plants, medicines, ailments!' Holding back his anger for a very brief while, he took off once again, 'You know what . . . I am throwing you three right here. Masjid not too far from here. Been here once before on my way to Nainital . . . know the maulvi sahib! Have risked my life and also that of these two friends by carting you three. You three can well be stuffed into some madrasa here or there, but what about we three, where the hell we go! The police will not be sparing us. Never ever before seen all this, not in these fifty years of my life!'

Arun continued driving, with Musarrat giving the needed directions, before braking in front of a mosque looking structure, situated under a sprawling tree. A huge lock dangling right on its front iron gates stood out, but before we could sit back, a maulvi's face peeped out from the grilled window. He recognized Musarrat mia, he raised his hand and asked us to come from the back door.

I wasn't too sure whether we boys were also supposed to get off the vehicle and follow the three men into the mosque but seeing me somewhat unmoving from the car interiors he lost his cool, once again that is, 'Off . . . Get off. Get off and come inwards with us. Hear what the maulvi going to say . . . he not looking his former self.'

The back iron door unlocked by the maulvi himself and then we followed him to the interiors. Nothing very much spread on the floor except for a couple of mats and a chair lookalike holding out a couple of Urdu akhbars. Looking about uneasily, he spoke of the tense times the small Muslim community of the town was going through, 'Only some old persons come here for nimaz. The police keeps a track of who coming and going . . . like you janabs here, they would surely get to know. I sent off my family to Barabanki because not sure what happens here. Not many Musalmaans here and I know two families in Bheemtal. Also know some sardars who very good to us Musalmaans but . . . '

And as Musarrat mia directly or indirectly asked the maulvi whether it will be safe to lodge us— three madrasa boys, the maulvi looked at him in a strange way. Yes, in a very obviously strange way, as though Musarrat mia was retarded and that's why couldn't understand what he was trying to tell—that is, the atmosphere is very unsafe for the Musalmaans, more so if the man or woman looked a Musalmaan! He'd repeatedly said that it would be more than risky for him to keep us. He had himself shifted his biwi and bacchas back to his native place, Barabanki, near Lucknow. He then went on to explain that he's not even able to serve us tea as there's no milk or sugar, 'So much tension . . . not bothered about food. At night one local eatery sends some food for me and that's it. Sometimes one or two Sardar families in Bheemtal send some fruit.' Suddenly as though some brainwave had hit him he looked somewhat less tense, 'If you people want I could talk to Singh sahib. He could keep these children in his outhouse. He has built a small house on the bypass and he will have no problem keeping Musalmaans with him. His construction sites have many Musalmaan labourers .I've seen several men wearing topis and kurtas. '

Before Musarrat mia could say a word, Arun vetoed the suggestion, 'No sawaal . . . in my Bareilly my Sikh and Hindu friends would keep them. No problem but we looking for a place where they could study and stay for months or years.'

The maulvi then came up with the next suggestion, that we drive further towards Nainital and then the big mosque near the Nainital lake could be a safe sort of refuge, which Musarrat wasn't sure of, 'We go driving another hour towards Nainital only to hear a no. You first ask the maulvis there if we could come otherwise too much waste of time and useless sort of tension . . . seen that mosque very near the lake!'

I know it was idiotic of me to scream out, 'My Dal lake is . . . '

I had to shut up and not say a word more of my Dal lake as their glares turned more than glares. Arun pulled me aside, and told me to keep shut, not a word more.

The maulvi dialled and re-dialled. Then gave up. His tone more than suggested that there stood out a dismal situation, 'Too many, too sipahis around. All keeping a watch on whose there or not there. All ask the useless type of questions. Get going from here before sipahis come here to question me!'

I had dared not ask a single question. Just kept my ears open, to get to know where we were being driven to. After a while, Arun looked exhausted and asked Afsar to drive till Bareilly and then they'd decide whether we go towards Lucknow or stay put in Bareilly at least for a couple of days. But Afsar said he was much too exhausted.

So Arun went on driving, talking about the control of the politicians over the police. If only father would be here to hear these talks, then he'd have realized that there was little point in packing me off to this killer land!

My thoughts were rudely intruded into, as Musarrat mia threw water from the bottle on Arun's face, drops of which fell on my shoulders. Arun looked irritated, screamed he wasn't asleep but needed tea. Almost simultaneously he braked near a dhaba, manned by two bearded men with topis atop their skulls. The dhaba looked deserted except for a stove chullah and a twisted pan atop it with the heady brew boiling, over-boiling ever so very lethargically. Not getting off from the car, perhaps as a precautionary measure, they looked out of the window and ordered tea and atta biscuits but the sellers came up with this, 'Only chai . . . all the atta biscuits those sipaiyyas took away. They took away the entire kanastar with them. Can't say a thing otherwise we be killed. We also going from here. Whoever stops here, stares at our topis and beards and then drives past by. No questions they ask, otherwise we ready to give any answers or explanations. They just stare at us, then get going as though we untouchables!'

Terrible watery concoction, the so-called chai, which we gulped down before the car picked up speed. This time Afsar behind the wheel; he was driving nervously as though not sure what lay ahead, along the same road which had taken us upwards. This time getting us back to Bareilly.

Quick decisions were made by the three men controlling our lives and destined turns. Arun decided to leave this car at his friend Satinder's workshop, and then take another car from there. Safer that way. And then Musarrat would take the three of us to Lucknow. Arun and Afsar to move towards some sort of a hideout, till things settled down or till the cops would have orders to chase several others who dared to lodge FIRs against the official killers of the day!

I was getting so very confused as they were coming up with so many names of places that Afsar and Arun were thinking of getting off to. Let me try remembering some of those names of those places they were planning to get to—Tilhar, Shahbad, Raeespur, Rampur, Faridpur, Kiccha, Ramnagar, Moradabad.

It was much later in the afternoon that we reached Satinder's workshop situated on the outskirts. We walked inwards to the workshop, sure that we'd be able to sit back in some sort of peace. Relief was short lived as some sort of paint work was on, with fumes spreading out. No, Satinder wasn't standing around with a paint brush in his hands but ordering two creepy looking characters, who were splashing red coloured paint on the doors and walls of the huge workshop.

Suddenly I remembered when we had painted the doors and walls of our Srinagar two-roomed dwelling in red! Father used to say that he must have been at some stage of his life in the Communist Party, because he was simply in love with the red colour, so much so that after visiting one MLA sahib's home who was from that CPI party, he decided to buy one tin of red paint. He called it Post Office red. How irritated mother looked, as he went about painting the window frames and the inner doors of our home in that PO red paint, telling us, 'You know he a big politician . . . Yousuf sahib's home all red coloured; this same red colour on his doors and windows. Not any red colour but PO red. This is what he was telling his friend who was sitting there. I went to Ibraheema's paint dukaan and asked him what's this PO red all what. He told me it's like the Post Office colour.'

Of course, my mother's anger didn't subside. Not even when the colour faded and turned pale. Now, for the last three or four years, nobody was really bothered about the home—how it looks!

My thoughts about my Srinagar home halted when Satinder's men put tea and a plateful of pakoras on the carved table in front of us—Sohail, Sultan, and I. Don't know how many pakoras we ate that afternoon—in seconds the big plate was without pakoras!

Through the glass door, saw Satinder gulping down tea, eating whatever was put on the plate on his office table. He looked so carefree. Why couldn't we three sitting on this side of the workshop look as carefree as him . . . why couldn't we laugh in that carefree way? I turned to see how Afsar, Arun, and Musarrat looked. They had just entered that office, wiping their faces and arms. They looked so tense, more so as they started talking to Satinder . The glass door stood in way so couldn't hear what all was spoken. The three didn't touch any of the snacks and namkeens on the stainless steel plates but yes, did gulp down many glasses of water. After five minutes the three coming out, with Satinder telling them that many a time some sarkari cars also come to his workshop so if they spot Arun's car parked right there, then big problem for everyone.

Some sort of relief spread out when he suggested that they park the car in his farmhouse at other end of the city. He even offered to give one of his rooms to Arun and Afsar to stay put till things would settle down.

But before he could utter any more, the two men declined saying that they are now thinking of heading with us towards Lucknow and then decide to return or not. As of now they can't leave Musarrat alone at this crucial time.

As the car took off towards the farmhouse, wanted to go to the toilet but didn't know to put across the urgency. Just when I couldn't control, screamed! Arun on the driver's seat, turned to tell me to hold on for some more minutes, but seeing me hold my stomach, he backed—back to Satinder's workshop, with me rushing inwards towards the toilets, but fell on a paint can . . . the red paint on the slippers and feet and also heavily drenched were the ends of the white pyjama on me . . . even in that condition I rushed towards the toilet. Walking out, realizing the huge paint spots I was leaving with every step I was taking.

Satinder frowned, seeing the marks spread out of the floor, Arun and Afsar looked livid, Musarrat mia tried to control his impatience, 'Now we get him new clothes otherwise the journeying will get tougher, very risky. Sipahis and thanedars might think these are blood marks and then we charged with murder!'

The only two persons who looked at me with some level of envy were Sohail and Sultan, whispering, 'Could have thrown some paint at us too . . . we'd get rid of these clothes. Been wearing these for so many days. Stinking!'

I stood back with tears in my eyes as Satinder rushed to his home to fetch his son's clothes. Tense, I stood in one of the inner covered sheds. Within ten or fifteen minutes he got back a huge bag, stuffed with a pair of shorts and a shirt and three pair of slippers. Shorts! How I do wear shorts and with that my legs getting uncovered!

No, never before I was made to wear shorts. Even two or three years back when it was very, very hot in our Srinagar, it had to be pyjamas or shalwar. That's a different matter altogether that I used to pull them up during the night. Last year I'd seen our neighbour's son Shafique in shorts going down the alley next to ours, and had immediately told Gulzar, who in turn told grandmother and she threw up her arms in utter dismay but mother and father quietened her, telling that his clothes must have shrunk, 'These days bad quality stuff . . . either fading away or shrinking.' Then before giving me those disapproving looks father had continued, 'Can you imagine any of our Kashmiri boys going around here in half clothes! Nah, nah, impossible! Shorts not for us, Kashmiris. Our children got to dress decently, fully clad.'

Now, me sitting with shorts on, and strange looking slippers which Arun insisted on calling 'floaters'. I felt strange, as though I am getting slowly but rather too surely transformed. Somehow I was angry with myself and also with these four men—how dare these people try to dilute or lessen my Kashmiri identity! How dare they!

Kept pulling at the shorts on me, till Musarrat mia commented, 'Think yourself lucky that you got these to wear . . . right now don't even have enough petrol money for the travel ahead and here you trying to undo!'

Don't know in which part of outer Bareilly the farmhouse was located, where the car was to be parked. Arun drove for many minutes, following Satinder's car. Finally, we entered that farmhouse. Arun parked his car at one side, close to the hedge but not before upsetting a bee hive and hell broke out. The bees attacked Arun and Afsar. The rest of us had managed to run inwards as fast as we could. Musarrat mia was still inside the car so he shut the windows and sat back. Satinder's gardeners and servants ran about with fire mashaals to scare the bees away before he could be retrieved from the car interiors. The cook—a young looking woman— made a paste of garlic and onion and turmeric, and gave it to them to put on the stings. And as the gardeners were explaining to them to rub the concoction as soon as possible, as it will pull out all the toxic poisons and with that lessen the pain, my thoughts went back to Imtiaz. How he would tell me about each and every plant and along with that about the leaves and flowers with their healing powers. What if he was alive then he would be himself plucking out flowers and leaves from the sprawling garden to this farm house and putting the paste on the bee stings. But then, I smirked to myself—if he was alive we wouldn't be running from there to here. By now we would have been lodged somewhere and not running around in this hapless- helpless- hopeless way.

The young cook, Sarla Didi, came again with more of that paste and insisted that it was applied immediately. Though she looked much younger than my mother but carried the same sort of concern. Yes, a concerned look on her face. And then kept telling us details of how last month her husband, who works as a maali here, was attacked by bees and if that was not enough he was also bitten by two stray dogs. Right now he's lying in the servants' quarters, but still not too sure to stay put here or go back to their village in Lalitpur. She's been talking non-stop of him.

Satinder entered the room well in time, for her talks to come to an abrupt halt. Though it seemed he'd heard some of her offloads, for he continued where she'd left and spoke of stray dogs terrorizing the locals. He even mentioned some woman minister's name who wouldn't let the municipality touch even one stray dog, no matter how many humans get bitten. He went on to say that the stray dog nuisance spreading in the entire belt, telling us two of his cousins died last month of rabies.

He wouldn't let us travel immediately in this condition. It was decided that Arun and Afsar would stay put in the farm house. Only Musarrat would take the three of us towards Lucknow and then get back.

He'd also arranged a car for our journey ahead.

Before leaving his place I asked him if I could pick up two of the notebooks kept right there in that room. He laughed in that carefree way before putting all the piled up notebooks in a cloth bag and handing me that bag. 'Take all . . . got them for myself but where's the time to write! Controlling the servants here is madness . . . getting blood pressure every single day . . . then hearing of these bites . . . either getting bitten by snakes or dogs or cats or bees or biting each other! Want to sell off everything here, to live in your Kashmir. So beautiful there. Been there only once long time back . . . went walking all around the Dal lake and those beautiful gardens and then even walked on and on till Charar.'

I wanted to cry out and tell him that's all a fairy tale of the past. There are so many stray dogs all over my Kashmir that walking alone or even in company of elders gets very difficult. So many of my school friends got bitten—Nissar and his cousin Nishat and also Zulfikhar and Iftikhar and Iqtidar. All been attacked by stray dogs.

Everybody looking fatigued and exhausted, more so, Musarrat mia. I even overheard him telling Satinder that he'd taken his huge risky responsibility of carting us to a safe destination. He was more than muttering, 'Before the Babri mosque destruction I couldn't be bothered but that destruction hit. Awakened me. If I don't do for my community children then who will! Not this government! All these fellows out to kill and kill more and more of us, so I got to protect my children. If I'd found these boys loitering around before 1992, I couldn't have really given a damn but all's changed for me now! Imagine me who used to not budge from that woman Munni's home, though ammi and abba used to send Shareef and his brothers Raheem and Kareem to fetch me but the way I used to shoo them off. Now all has changed. Ammi and abba must be seeing the changed me from the heaven up there!' I also overheard Satinder telling him about the 1984 riots which killed hundreds of sardars and how that changed him. He keeps guarded all the time.

Finally, we started. Musarrat mia driving an old Alto car and three of us sitting on the back seat. Though I wanted to sit on the front seat but he said that that could attract attention at the municipality chungi gates/check posts. I couldn't really understand what he meant by that, but things got clearer when police vehicles went past us. No they did not halt or made us halt but only slowed down, making checks with their eyes!

I could see sweat trickling down Musarrat's face. He hadn't driven very far when he muttered that he was finding it difficult to drive as the road lights are very dim and he wasn't too sure whether we were being followed. He'd even slowed down once or twice, to talk to Satinder or Arun or Afsar and then vetoed all suggestion of getting back. Instead, he told them that he knew of some family who lived in Shahbad—and we could stop there and maybe take one of their servants for the journey ahead. He had visited that family with his ammi and abba when he was studying with their son Quddoos at the Aligarh Muslim University ... many years back.

17 November—10 p.m.
This time not writing; sitting in the car. Now writing from Shahbad—from Hyderi sahiba's haveli.

He didn't have to ask more than one shopkeeper about the Alizai mohalla where Quddoos sahib lived. He pointed in the other direction adding 'Quddoos sahib ka inteqaal ho gaya. Bus ab begum sahiba hain.

Aur sab log guzar gai. Mirza sahib bhi.' (Quddoos sahib has died and so have other member of the family including his father, Mirza sahib. Only his mother, begum sahiba, alive.)

Musarrat mia was too taken aback, so didn't ask any details of the deaths. Drove till the dead end of the road and a crumbling structure stood still.

He looked about uneasily and kept muttering, 'So much changed! Where are the lawns and the fountains and the pehredaars / guards!'

He told us to stand near the front iron gates while he looked for some side way to get in. Finding none, he tried to rattle the loose looking rusted lock chained around it but though it brought along strange sounds but no movement from the inner quarters. Finally, one woman with head covered with a dupatta peeped out from the well covered veranda and then another face also peeped out from another end of the veranda. His 'As-Salam-Alaikum' brought one of the two women out of the peeping state, and closer to the gates. Coming up with a 'Walai-Kum-Salam' she seemed to be looking more and more confident—confident enough to be nearing the gates. He seemed to recognize her almost instantly but she took a while. *'Hyderi apa . . . hum Musarrat hain. Ammi aur abba ke saath aap ke iss haveli meai aaya thaa, bahut saal pehle.'* (Hyderi apa, I'm Musarrat. I had come here to your haveli many years back with my mother and father.)

She nodded and kept on nodding, while instructing the other woman—who had by then also picked up courage to walk towards the gates, to open the locks, and get us in.

We followed her inwards, into what seemed a hall full of photographs and chandeliers and old sofa sets. All old stuff. Even this lady must be in her late 60s .Yes, yes, she must be around my grandmother's age. Though my grandmother looked somewhat older but this lady had a firm and strong look to her, as though, she couldn't ever be defeated in life.

Before Musarrat mia could go on and go ahead to ask her about her son and husband she herself decided to tell us. In between, telling the servant woman to get us tea and something to eat.

Over rotis and egg curry we heard her tell him that Quddoos like his abba couldn't take the strain of the times. No, he couldn't take to the political upheavals. He tried to get some level of employment—sarkari or non-sarkari. He couldn't even go abroad because of the property here, though she kept telling him to go off to Saudi or Dubai but then his father would sit and weep for days. 'Then Mirza sahib had a heart attack, then heart failure. The same night goondas occupied our farm house and wouldn't vacate it. I threw off my burqa and went with Quddoos to collector sahib's office but he made us sit for hours. When he finally met me I told him that I am also the daughter of a collector sahib, he told me that all those old days are gone . . . he even asked me that why didn't we go and live in that Muslim land, that new country especially carved out for the Musalmaans!'

She kept telling us that night Quddoos kept sitting and smoking away. 'I knew he smoked but never in front of us. That whole night he smoked and smoked and then come morning he was nowhere to be seen. By the afternoon he had got along his friends and took them to the farm to attack the goondas occupying the farm house. These people carried no arms with them, whereas those goondas had guns and what not. They were booked as criminals but Quddoos and his friends were booked for terror activities and sent to a prison near Agra! My child couldn't take the strain and died in that prison . . . don't know because of torture or wounds . . . dead he was. I went, got my child's body and buried him here in our khandaan's qabristan. All's gone! The farmhouse taken . . . shops also taken by some minister's men . . . now they are even eyeing our qabristan. I'm alive, living on my pension. All servants gone, only Raeesan remains. She and I have nowhere to go except to Allah mia! Don't know what happens next.'

18 November—3 a.m.

Last night, when we didn't move or when she realized that we wouldn't be moving she didn't ask any of us any of those questions, instead asked Raeesan to put the daal on the gas stove and also to boil potatoes which herself cooked. I loved the way she kept relaying instructions to the servant woman, while sipping tea and together with that hearing Musarrat mia giving explanations why we would have to spend this night there. I think she's quite okay with our staying back and then she told us that she no longer meets many people. 'Though Mishra sahib's family living next door have been here from decades. Yes, years and years before my family came here from Farrukhabad but *now woh pehle jaise baat nahin rahi hai . . . bas doorr doorr sei salaam dua.* Can't talk to Mishra's children about any of the pogroms and riots or destructions taking place.

Nah, they don't like such talks. Mishra sahib's youngest daughter Nidhi who's doing some research work, starts arguing in that rude way, telling me how Muslim invaders destroyed all structures here in our Hindustan. Last time I gave it off to her, telling her that at least those conquerors destroyed buildings, not like today when human structures are getting destroyed. Now I only want to meet our Musalmaans but in the last four years the Muslim families I knew have left this place—Farooqui sahib's family moved to Lucknow and Hassan Hussain's family moved to some place in Saudi and even Taj sahib's sons have moved to Dilli.'

No, I'm not feeling sleepy. Yes, very, very tired but so tired that my eyes are rebelling as though not in that mood to shut. I can see her saying her nimaz on the jane- maaz/prayer mat she's spread out in the veranda. After all, that's where she said she will sleep after giving her room to Sohail and Sultan and the side study room to me and the hall to Musarrat mia.

I don't want to move from here. Feeling secure and safe. Tomorrow I will ask her if she could keep me and the two boys here . . . will look after her and she can keep us protected. Maybe I can call Gulzar here too, from Srinagar . . . why not! How to call father? Haven't seen her with a mobile . . . maybe she's hidden it, thinking that we might steal her phone or make calls.

Okay let me try sleep. Don't know what tomorrow brings along.

19 November—1 a.m.

So much to write . . . so much. I have this room to myself and there's this proper light . . . so much to write. From the window I can see out. Seeing her bent on the mats, praying and this time I can see even that Raeesan praying.

You know in the morning, while she was giving us chai, she looked towards Musarrat mia and asked him that why he looked so very tense. Though he had already told her about us and about him taking the re- sponsibility of taking us to Lucknow because he is himself not sure of his own life so how on earth he'd be able to take care of us , but till now he hadn't told her about Imtiaz getting lynched and how the cops have got after him after he put pressure on them to lodge an FIR against those killers who happen to be the henchmen of some top minister. While he was telling her all those details about Imtiaz's death she patted my head so very gently that I not just burst out but held her hand tight in that way of wanting anchorage . . . pleading for security, for that feeling of security. Don't know how words started tumbling out from my mouth, 'I want to stay here, with you here. I can even get my people from Kashmir here. Don't let me go from here.'

I don't know what all I said. And as she wiped the tears from my face, Musarrat mia got busy trying to tell her about me—how I landed from Kashmir to Uttar Pradesh!

She looked absolutely at ease, hearing the two words—Kashmir and Kashmiri. She kept patting my head, telling me that she has many books on Kashmir in her room, telling us that her walid (father) used to take them to Kashmir every summer but then her going there stopped when she married into this zamindar family who believed in only two hill stations—Mussoorie and Nainital . Kashmir was too far for them but whenever Kashmiri shawl-wallahs brought shawls and embroidered pherans, she would sit and talk to them for hours about Srinagar.

Even before I could say anything more, she told me that she would have been only too happy to keep me at her place but now halaats all too changed. She went on saying that she was nearing 70 years and if she dies then the goons roaming around would harm me. Raeesan also too old to even raise an alarm. Even if she does so, who will be there to listen!

After we sat there for don't know how long, she kept telling Musarrat to stay on with us for as many days as possible. She also told him that she had a revolver and even a gun with her.

We got up, only to move from one room to the other room, looking at the photographs hung on the wall and to go through the books she had brought out.

There was that heavenly silence here. Musarrat mia kept his mobile switched off and she and her maid didn't keep a mobile. Only a land-line which didn't seem to ring! Musarrat mia managed to dig out a chess player and while Sultan and Sohail went towards the courtyard, I went through the books—two books on Lalla Arifa in Urdu, one on the house-boats in English and many others on Avadh and also on the Freedom Struggle, also many issues of the Avadhi Punch magazine.

Only once during the entire day the landline rang. She told us it was from one of the friends who have moved to Lucknow; they asking her to be there for Muharram at the Bara Imambara, but she can't move from here because of the home and also because of Raeesan. And I liked her innocent little reply when Musarrat mia, rather too innocently asked her that who will look after her home when she has to go to Allah mia. She laughed a bit, quipped, 'Musarrat mia why don't you settle down here. I know your haveli must be big but sell it all off and settle here. You can drive down to Lucknow from here; only two or three hours drive from here.'

He was blunt. Told her that he has sold off most of his ancestral lands and now nothing much remains with him. 'Now only ruins remain, but to shift out would be difficult, though many Muslim families from Western Uttar Pradesh either sitting in fright like refugees or moving out.'

And as she once brought up the topic of his marriage, he tried to divert her attention by asking her to find a girl for him. She again looked glum and forlorn, 'Partition took away our best families from here. The cream gone. Who remains, remains in ruins. I hardly keep in touch with anyone, not even with my far-flung relatives in Aligarh and Farrukhabad. They must be having daughters and granddaughters but don't know who's where. After Mirza sahib and Quddoos passed away I'm also almost dead, but when you go to Lucknow meet my friends' families. Will give you their numbers. They would know many families there in Lucknow, meet them and marry someone.' Looking at us in that motherly way she added, 'You boys too young otherwise would have asked you to get married too!'

After hearing her say this, I suddenly felt all too grown up and as though all set to marry! Can't marry here. No, never. Has to be a Kashmiri girl who can understand my Kashmiri language, what I want to eat and how. Yes, yes, someone who looks a Kashmiri. Of course, father and mother will find some girl for me but how will I feed her and how will I look after her! See my condition, how I have to go from place to place. Really want to tell all this to my father. Don't know how he thought I will be all okay here. How he thought that I, a Kashmiri, will be accepted by these Indians when they hate us! How can I ever erase memories of the security men staring at us as though we were dogs or what. How dare they! They coming to my Kashmir to beat and thrash us. It's our land, we live there. Our stupid silly leaders have done nothing to help us. I want to tell father all this. I want him to come here and get me back... Seen the landline here. Will just ask her and then try father's number. I hope his mobile is still with him. I hope he's not sold it off or lost it or thrown it away into the Dal!

20 November—2 a.m.

I know I haven't written for the last several hours. I could have as I've this room to myself and the lights are on, and I had carried enough note books from that sardar sahib Satinder's table. I'm feeling very sad, shaken. After months saw the television news. Musarrat mia spotted the television placed in the hall and first he thought that it's some old discarded television set but when he switched it on it was working. Though black and white but blaring news alright. He kept changing channels and stopped at Al-Jazeera and then moved on to BBC . . . muttering all the while that many Indian channels are sold off so no correct news when it came to the Kashmir situation. We all gathered around the set, even Raeesan. Only Hyderi sahiba sat far away, in the next room, saying that she doesn't open this idiot box as it makes her feel very depressed.

When she was saying all that I couldn't really grasp or understand what she meant by all that but now I do. Most of the news was about my Kashmir. How after Burhan Wani killing, even mourners were getting killed by pellet guns. How hospitals were getting flooded by the blind or the semi blind. The killings going on, many killed each single day. Don't know whether my brother Gulzar killed or there! All mobiles and internet connections been down and down for weeks.

After hearing the news I asked if I could use her landline. She looked at me in that same motherly way and patted my head and told me I should treat her home as my own. I first wrote down toth's number on a piece of paper as my hands were shaking and unsteady with a strange sort of nervousness overtaking, with thoughts that he would be in severe stress in trying to save Gulzar from the killers stationed there. Then I sat down and tried and then tried many times but though the bell was going but nobody answering. I don't know what went wrong with my head as I started wailing. Musarrat rushed towards me and so did Hyderi sahiba. She almost scolding me, 'That's why I don't see news. You can't do a thing to stop all these killings. The only result is that you end up killing yourself with sorrow.'

We had to leave the next morning, but seeing my depressed state, they decided to postpone it by another day or two. Musarrat mia wanted to get out till the local market but then decided against it. Perhaps, fear or apprehension of the cops was weighing on his mind, not really leaving him in peace. It was so very obvious. Even while he was eating or talking or walking his mind seemed elsewhere.

The situation worsened by the evening. Two phone calls on the landline, of course, (as the only mobile around was Musarrat's and he had kept it switched off) were damaging enough for our anyway worn out nerves. After we were over with the evening tea and home made namkeens, the landline rang. Since no phone call could be heard that entire day so its ring rather too piercing. More than that, Hyderi sahiba's voice also seemed to be piercing enough. She sounded curt and almost scolding the caller and ended the conversation rather too abruptly. Muttering, 'Mirza sahib's people still not letting me live in peace. His younger nephew Naseer keeps calling from Lahore. Says he's very concerned about me but been telling him so many times that phone calls from Pakistan are not safe for me. All calls coming from Pakistan are tapped. And here I stay all alone . . . only Allah mia and this Raeesan and me. Been telling him not to call me every other week but he does so. Gives me so much blood pressure!'

Barely had she got over telling us all possible details to her dead husband, Mirza's relatives and how they are now eyeing this property, the phone rang again. This time too she looked very charged; perhaps, thinking her husband's nephew once again on the line. After the initial hello, she sounded rather subdued, telling the caller how her relatives and friends are visiting her from Lucknow.

Sitting back, she told us that it was a phone call from the Mishra household. 'Inquisitive women asking so much. . . following all the activities here! Have to give explanations who visit me or come here to stay!'

Suddenly Musarrat mia looked tense and hyper and though she kept telling him not to worry too much, he did look more than worried, telling her that he wouldn't want her to land in some mess because of our stay. She kept comforting him all the more with details of who all she'd fought with after the death of her husband and her son. 'Chief minister's own step brother wanted to grab this haveli but I wouldn't let him grab an inch . . . not easy to attack me. Of course, not to say that in today's Hindustan it's not difficult to destroy a Musalmaan but not me . . . very, very bad times for us. I feel another dark phase will spread out. It is already spreading out.

Something uneasy, something eerie in the air. Not the azaad Hindustan for whose azaadi we all fought for.'

That night I couldn't sleep at all. Something or say everything left me feeling very scared. What's in store for me—here or in my Kashmir! I think it's for the very first it hit me—that is, this combination of my being a Kashmiri and to top it a Musalmaan—will stand in way of my doing anything. The Muslim-bashers and Kashmiri-haters will hate me, will detest me, in stand in way of my doing anything. What all good will all this basic education get me! Nothing! I will not even earn enough to get going back to my Kashmir.

I sat up, walked out till the courtyard of this haveli where Neem trees stood out tall, their branches spreading out freely, as though they were all the same—nah, none of the Hindu or Muslim Neem trees! Though of course, I hadn't ever seen Neem trees growing in my Srinagar so that way these trees are non-Kashmiris, but because they are not my Chinars and not my Kashmiri trees so would I harm them! No way. Insane to even think of this insane thought!

I saw Hyderi sahiba sitting under one of the Neem trees, quietly crying or sobbing. Suddenly seeing me, she tried to regain her posture, but it was somewhat late. To worsen matters, Musarrat mia had also stepped out, perhaps for a breather and he too looked somewhat taken aback seeing her cry. At first he looked towards me, as though I had said something hurtful to her, but when she said that she sits and cries under this Neem tree every single night, then of course, the whole scenario stood changed.

The remains of that night were spent with the three of us—she and me and Musarrat—sit right there. First in complete silence and then she broke the silence—started off by telling us her absolute fascination for the Neem trees. Quite obviously I thought she was going to start off listing the health benefits to the Neem trees. In the Dilli madrasa I used to see the maulvis with those big fat hideous looking 'datoons' sticking out of their mouths before they would go throwing out the muck from their mouths—a combination of the saliva and the watery-juicy drops of the Neem tree branch. Then had come along Imtiaz who would drive me mad talking of what all the Neem tree and all its offshoots could do to settle all our ailments—be it related to purifying the blood supply to settling acnes and boils to also settling teeth and the gums. But to my utter surprise she dragged along those bygones from her life. How she used to meet her neighbour's son under the Neem trees growing in great numbers in her father's Farrukhabad home. Yes, she described those meetings and how those trees provided all possible privacy. Their meetings went on unnoticed for months but when the branches had to be pruned blood flowed out from the branches. The gardeners told them that Jinns and Jinnats lived on those trees and by mistake one of them got hurt or wounded. So terrified was her father that for days he said his nimaz under those trees asking for forgiveness and also shifted house—to another house in another corner of that town, 'My meetings with Tabish Hussaini stopped. And when I mustered enough courage to tell my father that wanted to marry him he threw a fit—we Sunni so how on earth can you marry a Shia! That was the end of it. I was married off to Mirza Sanaullah . . . very unhappy but then couldn't have done a thing. Many years later I had tried to find Tabish but his family seemed to have shifted to Canada. Whenever I feel very restless, these Neem trees try to settle my restlessness, taking me back to those days, to those nights when Tabish held me tight in his clasp, as though he and I wouldn't ever part ways but what's left back! What's become of all those years . . . all those dreams . . . all gone away for ever!'

I couldn't understand this Shia–Sunni thing. Nor did she want to explain. Probably thought I would know or should know. Though in Srinagar we were told about Tibetan Musalmaans—those Tibetan refugees who lived in newly constructed homes near the steps leading to the Makhdoom sahib dargah. They were all Muslim families but kept to those themselves, no never did they near us. Once or twice I had accompanied my grandmother and mother to those Tibetan shops where I saw them making embroidery on scarfs and pherans, but no talks about Shias or Sunnis. Yes, yes, I remember father telling someone that he had many Shia friends in Kargil.

In the morning, there was no occasion to ask her about this Shia–Sunni thing as she was making baqarkhanis—(rotis made with maida atta kneaded in milk and creamy concoctions and ghee) for us, to be taken along with us to Lucknow—my next destination. And when Musarrat mia commented on the smell of that pure ghee, she let out another little offshoot to it—'till this summer we had two cows tied right here in this compound but with news of killings taking place of us Muslims with the cow pretext, I decided give them to the local mandir. In fact, Raeesan's idea that we shouldn't get into any useless musibat, so we gave them off . . . donated them. This ghee stored for months, now making these rotis for you all to carry. *Khuda janai ab kab milaingai!* (Don't know when we'll be able to meet again)

22 November—3 a.m.

We had to move from here yesterday, but Musarrat mia didn't want to even move out of his room. When Hyderi sahiba kept calling out for nashta, he said he's worried what lies ahead in Lucknow or when he gets back to his ancestral place.

The whole day Hyderi sahiba kept telling him to shift to Lucknow, but he looked unsure. She went on repeating that even if he's lynched or attacked in a place like Lucknow, there'll be 10 to 20 persons who could stand as witnesses but not so in a place where he's all alone!

He'd kept quiet all through her long and short lectures and after what seemed hours he just came out with a simple sentence— *'har haal mai maar diya jaonga!'* (will be killed under any of the circumstances.)

And when she tried to argue further, that there'd be chances of him getting protected in a place like Lucknow or Dilli or even at her little township of Uttar Pradesh, he suddenly got up with a big Uff coming out from his mouth along with loads of saliva, 'You seriously think any one from the crowds will come out to protect me or to be a witness in the courts! Nobody! All will be either beaten to pulp in the police lock up or bought over with the hordes of money in those lockers of these men. Let's see what to do with my life!'

Then out of the blue he went on telling her and, of course, we three also couldn't possibly shut our ears, how in his younger days he had started going out, night after night, to all sorts of places, for dance and drinks and what not! And though his parents and sister knew about his 'outings' but couldn't stop him for fear of his anger. But something hit him after seeing the destruction of the Musalmaan community in his region and he's now doing every little bit he can do for his community. Because of that inner calling, he was undertaking this entire exercise of carting us to a safe place. He then started pacing in a strangely charged way, 'But couldn't save that one child Imtiaz. That poor child killed. Now I'm getting hounded for lodging the FIR!'

I kept on wishing that Hyderi sahiba would ask us to stay put at her home forever. Stay put! There was something different about her and her home. Here, in this home, there were no don'ts. She would be saying her nimaz but not once asked any one of us to say the nimaz or recite any of the ayats/religious text.

And last evening when I was once again looking towards the telephone instrument, she asked me to feel free to dial as many telephone numbers I wanted to. After weeks I smiled and kept smiling; though from what I'd seen and heard on the television screen I knew too well that no mobiles were working in and around Srinagar yet I couldn't resist the temptation of trying and re-trying toth's number. Apprehensions hitting when it went un-answered. Hyderi sahiba saw me looking glum and then when she asked the other two boys if they want they could try their parents' mobiles from her landline but they simply shook their heads. She had asked them yes-terday too but they'd sat all tight and tense. This time again they looked very tense—Sohail said in that flat emotional-less voice that he has no ammi and abbu—*Allah mia ke paas chalei gai.* (mother and father gone to God)

And the other boy Sultan said that his people have no mobiles.

There was an ongoing silence in the room, till she broke the silence—telling him that even she doesn't keep a mobile. She went to tell him that she she's never bought one. She hates mobiles!

To which he said somewhat shyly, 'They want to keep one but can't be-cause no rupees with him. At times no rotis too. That's why they sent me off. Amma cried, she didn't want me to be sent away but abbu forced his way, saying that I will die of hunger if I wasn't sent to the madrasa. No, they didn't send me there for any *likhai-padai* (studies) but to get many rotis to eat!'

I think Musarrat mia and Hyderi sahiba knew this fact; that most of the children sent to the madrasas are sent for those two meals a day, or as they call it here in Uttar Pradesh for that savior daal-roti. That's a different story that even getting that essential *khurakh* (basic essential food) was difficult to get in many madrasas.

First time in all these months of my being sent away from home I felt I could talk *khul ke*, frankly and openly, not under the various don'ts that the Dilli maulvis inflicted on the children in the form of 'tehzeeb'. What tehzeeb or culture! When stomachs are rumbling . . . empty. When there is that constant 'darr' (fear) of getting attacked by the goondas on the prowl, hitting with cricket bats and stumps on our head because we looking Muslims with skull caps on our heads!

All along the way to this place, Musarrat mia had kept telling us to remove the topis; not just remove them but not even hold them in our hands. His nervousness had accelerated after Imtiaz's lynching.

Last night when Musarrat mia announced that tomorrow we got to leave early morning, she said she'd been hoping we would stay somewhat longer, till things settle down!

And much along the expected strain he snapped back, 'They wouldn't ever change. Only worsen!'

4

A Somewhat Peaceful Phase

30 November—2 p.m.

Writing after several days. Didn't feel like. Don't feel like living here. This place called the Centre for Islamic Studies, is also some sort of a madrasa-cum-school.

After Hyderi sahiba's haveli, all this looks useless. Why I'm here! Somewhat better than those earlier two madrasas, but more or less the typical type of talks of gunah, shaitan, and what not! But yes, much better than those two places. Many more books, some English books, and several on Science, History, and Geography. Some sort of a semi-library stands out, all these books were donated by the former taluqadars of the area. And one can read and write as much as one wants to, no restrictions on that.

Musarrat mia left the three of us here, at this Centre. Two maulvis were sitting in a bare room. They told him that he needn't worry one bit about us, provided we do 'no shaitani, should keep the shaitan far away from us.' Here, mobiles and transistors not allowed. They also told him they have one or two computers, but only for the older boys who were doing higher studies in Islamic Studies. They also made it very clear that we would be given two meals a day but no breakfast because no funds with them. If we are very poor, then they can give us gur-channa and a small cup of cheeni-walli-chai (sugary tea) and that too, because they have some taluqadar sahib's zakat money left with them.

Musarrat mia kept nodding. He telling us that if things turn somewhat better, he'd come to meet us, but we shouldn't wait for him. Also, in case Hyderi sahiba's friends get in touch with us or come to meet us, then we should meet them. Yes, yes, he gave us his mobile number but kept on repeatedly telling us and also the two maulvis that he should be called only if there is some emergency, otherwise not, because he's not sure of his own survival.

The Diary of Gull Mohammad. Humra Quraishi, Oxford University Press. © Oxford University Press India 2023. DOI: 10.1093/oso/9789391050269.003.0005

What emergency will be in this place where nothing happens! On the first day itself we had to be up at 5 a.m. and then say nimaz in the veranda, though I saw Sohail and Sultan walk to the hall situated in the centre of a courtyard of this building. Here all the washing of the face and arms and feet for the 'wazoh' done with cold water. No water heating rod or anything like that. Didn't even expect hot water facility here—around four hundred children and each child living with the basics—three sets of kurtas-pyjamas and two sweaters and one pair of socks. The slightly well-to-do boys wrapping mufflers around their necks and also putting on sneakers. When I asked Shaaz, where he got his shoes from, he told me that he collected enough money from the last Eid so that he could buy them from his 'Eidi' money. And yesterday when I complained about the cold water and the cold breeze combination, he told me to shut up and wait for the summer to hit when hot *loo* winds would be more than hitting. He told me there aren't any coolers here, though for his Golaganj home his parents had bought one cooler because last summer his sister had fainted, not once but twice. Why? Because of the temperatures and the doctor sahib had told his father that even a second-hand cooler would do to save her.

Thought Shaaz is from an 'okay' family because he has biscuits with him which he buys from the little shop situated at one end of the campus. No, no breakfast is given here. Those of us, including me, who have no means at all to buy even a packet of biscuit, are given a handful of channas and gur. At times chai in very small mugs.

I offered channas and a part of the gur piece to Shaaz which he promptly grabbed from my hand and in lieu of that he placed a biscuit on my palm. Only one biscuit and not two. This, when I gave him almost half the gur piece with me.

After breakfast, we went to the classrooms and started off reciting the Quran Paak. Though the boys and I seem to have learnt all the ayats by heart, even then the maulvi insists we go on and on. Just don't ask me why. Once or twice I tried to gather enough courage to tell the maulvi sahib if he could read a passage from the Quran and explain to us the real meaning to those verses but after seeing the frown spread on his face I'd sat back, muttering all those verses again and yet again. In between seeing my class fellows bending rather too pathetically in that ongoing way, with hunched backs reciting for hours.

The lunchtime is the only relief. Round thick rotis along with watery gosht salan. The first day I could see potatoes pieces also swimming in that salan. Then nimaz and then rest time . . . that's the time I loitered around in the garden—unkempt but full of Neem trees and many other trees. That's when I thought of Hyderi sahiba and wanted to talk to her. I asked Shaaz if he or any of the boys carried any mobiles with them and they laughed nervously, 'You want us to get slapped by maulvi Aleemuddin!' Shaaz even went on to tell us the details of the two mobiles at his Golaganj home—his ammi's and abbu's. And how he uses them all day once he's home for any of the holidays. But here absolutely no; it is unthinkable to even think of mobile phones!

Though the sight of the corner shop is more than beckoning, but where the five rupees to even think of buying a biscuit packet. Asir nimaz followed by the maghrib nimaz, and then time for the evening meal—rotis and daal, followed by reading. And then time to sleep.

The routine seems unchanging. I'm feeling caged and have been chanting sabr. Sabr!

3 December—4 a.m.
Yesterday Aleemuddin sahib was going across the Gomti Bridge to pick up 'galla'/grain from some outlying mohalla or colony, and he took Shaaz and me with him in the rickshaw to help him lift the sacks of the grain. The rickshaw puller stopped on the banks of the river as he couldn't stop coughing and throwing up.

We got off the rickshaw and walked towards river. It was smelling. All over filth and dirt, and on the sides there were lots of vegetables growing. It was all so very dirty. Nah, nothing like my Kashmir. I tried to tell maulvi sahib and Shaaz about my Dal lake, but they didn't seem too interested.

The rickshaw puller's cough wouldn't stop . . . poor man looked so weak. Maulvi sahib looked much hassled, and I think, hungry too, because he looked rather too longingly at the vegetables growing along the Gomti banks. Though he seemed to have controlled his hunger pangs, not Shaaz. And when I saw Shaaz pull out carrots, all too set to start off nibbling them, I held his hand and showed him the creatures crawling along the roots. Also, rather too spontaneously, I started talking about our Kashmir's floating vegetable gardens and vegetables growing on them. Maulvi sahib overheard some of those details and thought I was describing some locale plucked right out of his visions of the Paradise. And when I insisted that these floating gardens do exist in my Kashmir's Dal lake, he at first couldn't really believe a word of this and when I repeated all those details to the floating vegetable gardens, he said that he would try it out in his village pond. Poor man kept asking me—will it work, will it work? And looked very disappointed when I told him that I had read somewhere that these floating gardens were found only in one other place in the whole world—and that is somewhere in the Mexico city. Yes, yes, I remember those details—there they are called Chinampas—the floating gardens! The Chinampas, floating gardens in lake Xochimilco to the south of Mexico City.

His excitement didn't seem to subside. Like a child he asked me how to make those floating gardens. He looked so earnest, as though he could start off making the floating gardens there and then, on the banks of the Gomti. I told him whatever details I could remember—I told him that these floating gardens on the banks of the Dal lake, in my Kashmir, are made of long strips of matted roots of reed-grass, which along with the adhering soil, are tied tightly to each other, superimposing one strip over another. Then the tied strips are actually floated on the water. These strips function like ordinary soil, even though they have no sub-soil to rest and produce vegetables in great abundance.

5 December—4 p.m.
Been ill for the last one day. Very high temperature. I think I caught a chill that day on the rickshaw ride. Yesterday I couldn't even walk till the toilet—it is anyway situated outside, across the veranda. Maulvi Aleemuddin had got along a hakeem who told me to rub some ointments on my chest and then at night I was given two extra *kambals* (blankets)— especially got out from the store room. Today morning when the hakeem again came with the maulvi sahib, he asked me how did I, a Kashmiri, survive the harsh winter of my home town. Silly man didn't seem to know that we have kangris and so much of warmth inside our homes. Couldn't really argue with them nor could I give them a list of things to beat the cold, but all that I could say is that I wanted a pheran. Yes, yes, our pheran, because that alone can provide warmth to the body. Maulvi sahib looked around and asked hakeem sahib if he knew of some place in Lucknow where pherans are available. His answer made me feel hopeless because

he said that till last winter he could see many Kashmiri shawl sellers, but this winter none, as the police hounds and troubles them. What!

Shaaz tried to calm me and told me that he'll try to make maulvi sahib talk to his father because in their Golaganj mohalla Kashmiri shawl sellers take rooms on rent in the winter season.

After *zohar nimaz*, early afternoon—lunch time. Shaaz got rotis and a small bowl of daal and also the news that he had spoken to his father who would be coming over this evening. Let's see when his father comes and whether he will be carrying a pheran for me.

If I feel better, I will also walk across to the office to try and talk to my father. Maybe, the lines are okay. Will ask Shaaz's father, what news is there about my Valley . . . my home, my Kashmir!

Will write later. Been feeling very weak. No, no kehwah. Here they don't even understand what kehwah is all about!

5 December—11 p.m.
Shaaz's father looked like a gentle, kind man. Shaaz had told me that he is a qasai/butcher, so I was imagining him to be harsh or brutal looking, but he spoke so very gently while making me sip that yakhni he had got along. He also got along a pheran. No, he didn't hide the fact that it was an old one—his own, which he had bought two winters back from a Kashmiri shawl seller. Poor man took pains to explain to us, all possible details to that the shawl seller, Bismillah Shah, who used to come down every winter and take up a room on rent in the building across his home but no sign and nor any news of him this winter. He said that he tried his mobile but no connectivity in the Valley.

And before I could even ask him about the news on television about my Kashmir, he himself told the small assembly gathered around—Shaaz, Shareef, Sohail, Sultan, Abid, Hussain and Jaffar —that things are very bad in the Kashmir Valley. No phones working, no internet, no khabar, no news, no means to find out who's alive or gone.

The yakhni and pheran combination did help, feeling somewhat better but have told maulvi Aleemuddin that I'll not be able to attend the classes. Though he didn't look too happy, he didn't say a word. Sometimes he looks quite okay and somewhat kind.

I'm looking at the faces of these boys sleeping around me, on worn-out cotton mattresses spread over mats. I have been lying awake for more than an hour, been thinking of Gulzar and my home, how we played on the steps leading inwards to the rooms, where mother would be cooking and father sitting reading or talking to us in that ongoing way. Don't know whether I will see them in this lifetime or up there, in Jannat!

6 December—1 p.m.
I woke up coughing in the morning. My chest still somewhat heavy with congestion, yet I insisted on walking till the office. The two maulvis sitting in the front room looked somewhat startled—perhaps, because of the pheran on me and Shaaz's muffler around my head. I told them I wanted to try my father's number but seeing a lock on the dial of the telephone instrument, I realized that to get it unlocked I would have to walk in, further into Aleemuddin sahib's office. There he was seated with the hakeem sahib discussing the political halaats in the city—how the karsevaks and the Hindutva men had broken the Babri masjid way back in 1992 and how he's been deeply affected from that day. He kept saying that today—6 December—is the most painful day for him. More painful than 10 December when his son was killed in police firing on the protestors—all those who were protesting against the destruction of that mosque.

Seeing me, both the men looked more bewildered. More so, when I told them that I wanted to talk to my father —the whole night I had been only thinking about him, my mother, and brother.

'Let me try. Maybe, maybe the connectivity is there.'

The ring went through. And I could hear my father's voice. As he kept saying 'hello . . . helloo . . . hellooo . . . hello', I couldn't speak a word. My voice wouldn't come out. My throat felt chocked and blocked but yes, I could hear him—coming up with one sentence after another. In between it all I could also hear Gulzar and mother's voices. They are all speaking together.

I started coughing and then crying. All I could say that I wanted to be back home . . . home . . . home!

Maulvi sahib took the phone from my hand and tried to explain to my people how I landed in Lucknow and that I was well and safe and also gave the office number. He tried to tell father to call another time or day because my cough was bad and that's why I couldn't talk. I tried to snatch the receiver back from his hand, trying my best to say that maybe there's no connectivity tomorrow or the day after, so I'd speak or hear them now but by then the phone was disconnected. Maybe father was as tense and emotionally nervous as I'm.

I sat back, sobbing. Continued to sit there till about the time maulvi sahib and hakeem and the other two maulvis said that they were going till the GPO/Lucknow's General Post Office—for a protest meeting which is held year after year since 1992. They were locking the office. They were not taking the students because of the news around this time is that the police would use pellet guns on the protestors . . . kill or blind them!

I walked around for some time and then lay on the mattress. Sat up when Shaaz and two or three other boys asked me about pellet guns. I told them about Gulzar's one eye gone by the pellets fired around my home. Told them all I knew of the killings going on in my Kashmir.

Feeling very sad. Now don't want to talk to anyone about anything at all. Moved quietly at the other end of the room and took out this diary. Let me see how much I write. Not much, as images of my home, are standing out, in front of my two eyes.

6 December—10 p.m.

Don't know what time these maulvis got back from the GPO protest. It's only around maghrib nimaz time when the sun was setting that Ehsan— the little boy from Etawah came in, and asked me if I knew how badly wounded those person were, who'd gone for that protest meet. As I sat up to hear more details from him, Shaaz and Jabbar also walked in and started offloading how the police lathi charged and used tear gas to disperse the unarmed protestors. Maulvis back but very upset. Two of them—Qamar and Samar—had suffered fractures and Aleemuddin sahib's shervani was torn.

No dinner was cooked that night. And when I told Shaaz I was feeling very hungry, he walked towards the top shelf and slipped a biscuit packet in my hand. That's it. Nothing was cooked as everyone was very sad.

Now all are sleeping. I am looking at their faces—lined, tense, and upset. Ehsan must be only eight years old, but his face was looking so drawn—they were telling me that his entire family of eight siblings and parents had died last year because of TB, and he is the only survivor. Hakeem sahib keeps giving him many medicines and also lots of crushed Anaar and Amrood leaves. He says these leaves are good for health.

Ehsan always looks so sad. No one from his family alive.

My family alive but so far away.

After many hours, all I did was to keep chanting sabr and then my eyes closed.

7 December—5 a.m.

The sun is shining somewhat. Out but not really. Nah, I don't have a wrist watch on me but know the time either by seeing the big clock on the wall or else seeing the sun's rays. I know it's not very accurate, but I can have some idea to the time passing away by seeing the changing patterns in the sky.

Only last week, Shaaz told me two months back his watch got spoilt as it accidently fell in the bucket full of water. His father refused to buy him another one, saying that their business was not doing too good, so it's then one of the older boys here told him how the sun's light can relay the time of the day.

7 December—7 p.m.

Too much talk here of how the police did not allow the protestors to hold a meet at the GPO. Maulvi sahibs looking all very upset, discussing the 'halaats'. No classes were held. I am anyway exempted from the classes till my cough settles down.

The entire day I have been seeing hakeem sahib coming and going with his bag, maybe treating these three maulvis.

Was certain he'd ask about my cough but he didn't. Don't know why. Somehow felt bad about this. He should have asked me.

I walked towards the back side where thick shrubbery stands out and thought of trying out the leafy concoctions to settle the cough. Tried my best to think of the names of all such plants that Imtiaz used to talk of. Yes, those leaves of Tulsi, Amrood, Neem, and Loung (clove). Though many shrubs, plants, and trees stood out, I couldn't really make out what's what. Suddenly what caught attention were long fleshy leaves with tiny little reddish-whitish spots on them. They looked fascinating. Decided to pull out a few and put them in my room in the empty oil *sheeshee* (glass bottle) and place it on the top shelf but the minute I tried to pull out those fleshy green leaves, I felt a terrible burning sensation in my palms and fingers. I came running back and there stood the cook, Zahid Zubair, looking at my hands and shouting aloud. His shouts not directed towards me but towards that lame man, Shahanshah, who doubles as a gateman cum gardener cum errand boy, telling him that he should have destroyed and burnt these poisonous plants, before they kill any child. The hakeem also rushed towards me, saying these are all very *zehrela* poisonous plants and should be burnt immediately.

Before waiting for a nodding approval from the maulvis, this cook Zahid Zubair rushed towards the kitchen and rushed back and sprayed kerosene oil and struck as many match sticks as he could on those zehrela plants. Within minutes that shrubbery stretch was reduced to ash. In the backdrop, the cook, detailing the poisons tucked in the folds of those leaves.

Then the maulvis directed their anger at me—why the hell did I go towards that patch, that too, when I'm ill and unable to even attend a single class. And when I told them about my now dead friend Imtiaz telling me how certain plants and their leaves and flowers cure all colds and coughs, the cook smirked—telling the hakeem sahib to retire as they have this new hakeem sahib with them!

Nobody laughed or even tried to, because almost immediately maulvi Aleemuddin nodded and said in that firm way—even till this day he starts his day with Amrood leaves. He then asked me to follow him. He went towards the outer stretch to this complex and there at one corner stood out several Amrood trees together with Shareefa, Neems, Bel Pathars. And also turmeric, garlic, onions, and ginger growing in great abundance in the huge sprawling stretch.

I asked maulvi sahib if I could look after these plants and trees. He said that he was doing so but now I could help him but no plucking of too many leaves at one go.

He told the maulvis and the boys that they should plant many more saplings. Once again the cook butted in, saying that in this cold nothing can grow. He was snubbed almost immediately; this time by the hakeem—'*Bahaar aeigee* . . . another two months and Spring will be here! Plant as many trees as you wish to and Inshallah all will grow.'

I kept rubbing my hands as the itch was growing, so much so that I rushed towards the kitchen shed to ask the cook how to contain the red patches and the itching. He was busy kneading the atta and plucked out a little bit from the kneaded atta and asked me to rub it on the red patches. And then he also put lots of cold water in a degchi and asked me to dip my hands in it. Worried that the cold and congestion could worsen, I declined. He then added mustard oil to it and asked me to dip the hands once again.

Some relief. Whilst I was dipping my hands, one of the boys came running to say that there's call for me. Must be father . . . must be my father. I went running but by then it got disconnected. I kept sitting next to the phone till the evening but it did not ring again.

I tried but the bell went ongoing . . . unanswered.

Deadened and weak I lay down. Didn't sit up. Not even when the two rotis and daal arrived—that Shaaz had got me on stainless steel platter.

Why was I still so terribly restless! Maybe because I wasn't from here. Not my soil, not my place, not my watan.

8 December—8 a.m.

Since morning I am up but not really. Been looking at my hands . . . looking somewhat better but not all okay. Though the red patches have dimmed and the itching lessened.

You know at times when father used to see the lines on my and Gulzar's palms, he would turn towards mother and quietly say that there are too many lines on my palm and too few on Gulzar's. Then I didn't really understand or even tried to understand what he meant, but now I think I can! In fact, one day he had got back from some peer sahib who'd told him that times would be getting very tough and difficult. Then, he had sat seeing his own palms . . . spreading them out in a strange way towards the sunshine, as though studying all the lines and patterns on his palms. I had also overheard him telling mother that one big doctor had also come to the peer sahib's dwelling to discuss his problems, but the peer sahib refused to talk to him, and all that he did was to take off the doctor's wrist watch and kept fiddling with it. Giving the watch back to the doctor, he gestured to the doctor to get going. When the doctor asked when to come again, he'd said. 'Never. Now your life will take you much ahead. I have settled the very pace of your life. You will travel to Vilayat and be there.'

Don't know why I'm thinking of all this here. Where is the watch on me, who will take me to Vilayat, where are the peer sahibs here!

14 December—10 p.m.

It's getting bitterly cold. Someone had come and donated some *kambals*, but we couldn't get any of those. Those were given to the small children,

who use the smaller side-room. Can hear one of them crying at night—
ammi, ammi . . . till the other boys quietened him.

Two of the boys of my room complained about me that I keep the lights
on for too long at night. I told the maulvis that I feel scared—though that
is a big fat lie. Maulvis believed me and said to ward off the shaitan that
is scaring me, frightening me, I should recite the Ayatullah Kursi and all
fears will go away.

I want to write as much as I can; restlessness settles down somewhat.

15 December—5 p.m.
Father's call came today early morning. I could hear the maulvis
screaming excitedly, calling out for me, as I sat in the sun coughing.
Maulvi Aleemuddin's voice was the loudest, 'Your abbu from your
Kashmeeer . . . from your Kashmeeeer!'

I came rushing but after salaams couldn't utter a word more. Nor could
he, because my mother had taken the phone from him and started off by
telling me that I shouldn't get worried if I don't get to hear from them because the phone lines are down. Mobiles not working one bit. This time
they were calling from one far-flung relative's office who works for the
governor sahib, but he will not allow them to come anywhere near his
place any more, otherwise he will be off his naukri. She went on saying
that they are all well . . . all okay. Gulzar can see by that one eye. She asked
me how was Lucknow, do I go out, what studies are going on? I wanted to
talk to Gulzar, but they had not got him. Told me he was at home. It is not
safe for little boys to be seen outside . . . too much firing on. Father took
the phone and told me that they will call whenever the lines are opened
and that I should study very hard so that I get work. He also gave big hints
that I don't talk against the hukumat as even phone people are hearing.
Words along the strain that linesmen are attached to the phone lines. By
this time the line got disconnected.

I sat back and kept sitting the entire day. Now, as the sun going down
that Shaaz came in and told me that tomorrow 10 or 12 boys are going to
some person's home for Quran Khwani—recitation of the Quran.

Would I come along with them?

No, I told him. I was very worried about my people back home in
Kashmir. I wanted to earn some money for them so that I could get back,
but this way I could see my life going nowhere. All is waste here.

He kept arguing that going to some rich person's home for Quran Khwani will get us new clothes and good food. Sitting here what good will come our way!

16 Decemeber—8 p.m.

I got ready rather early as ten of us had to leave by 9 p.m, to one rich doctor's home—that heart specialist doctor sahib's family had to send a car to fetch us and take us to his home in Gomti Nagar to read the Quran and then have lunch and be dropped back.

A big van arrived only after 11 a.m. and after an hour or maybe more we arrived at that sprawling kothi. Like a herd of sheep or cattle, we were taken to the kitchen garden side of the kothi and given one mat to sit on. And after we had gone on and on reading the Quran, we were taken to another end of the kothi—a cemented patch near the garages and given a rationed supply of food—qorma in two small bowls and about ten big thick maida rotis called naans. That's it. Nobody from the family even bothered to come and meet us. We were left at the mercy of the servants hovering around, who later put us back in the van and sent back.

My cough worsened and all through the way back I gave those dagger looks at Shaaz. What good was that rich Muslim family for children like us, when they didn't even bother to come out and talk to us and ask us about our *haal chaal*, our halaats!

I felt cheated and very angry!

At least Balli and Satinder and Arun seemed earnest and genuinely concerned about us, about our welfare and well-being.

As soon as we got back—it was almost asir nimaz time—maulvi Aleemuddin helped us get into the hall for the nimaz. Then he asked me whether I was okay with where we were sent. Like a child he kept on talking away that we should feel so honoured that such a well-known heart specialist of Lucknow had invited us. I couldn't take it. I told him why we children are getting used! Our poor parents or whatever re-mains of them send us here to these madrasas so that we can get two rotis to eat and from here we have been sent here and there so that we get another two rotis to eat. I don't know what all I went on saying, and in that angry mood, walked back here to the room, started scribbling in this diary.

Till now nobody of this city has called me and the rest of the children for dinner or lunch, nor got here any of the food stuff for us. One could say it was the first outing for us!

I think I spoke out too much. But all these things have been troubling me so much.

16 December—11 a.m.
No, no food for me. The boys have all slept off, even Shaaz, who at first looked about somewhat uneasy, then stared at me, throwing those angry glances towards me. Later, he put two *kambals* on himself and snuggled under them.

I don't know whether I did the right thing or the wrong thing, but I was speaking out, loud and clear. Maybe I shouldn't have said all that, because I have to stay put here. And it is a safe refuge, where nobody threatens to oust me because I am a Kashmiri. Imagine, out of the four hundred boys I am the only Kashmiri! At least, I am not called a Pahari here.

Don't know what should I do? Should I go to Aleemuddin sahib's room right now and apologize or wait till the morning. He should be up at dawn for the nimaz. You know, these boys were telling me that he says his nimaz all night, so I should go now but then he might get too shocked.

17 December—11 p.m.
What a day! Early morning I did go to his room, but he pretended as though he busy seeing some papers kept on his takht. I kept sitting on the edge of the takht, and after about twenty minutes, he raised head and said that I should start attending the classes. I told him I was feeling upset for being rude last evening, but the way that doctor sahib's family treated us as though we were labourers got there. Suddenly he got up and started walking around and then sat back and asked me to leave. I wasn't sure whether he wanted me to leave this Centre or his room.

Go where!

I stood outside his room. Not sure what to say or do. Though I had taken down Musarrat mia's mobile number but calling him and then saying what! Maybe he had still kept his phone switched off, but even it was on and even if I could get to talk to him, what the hell could he do for me. He had already risked his life and that of his friends, trying to cart us till here. He could have sold us at some mandi or market place where children are sold very openly! Where do I go from here! I kept standing and looking at the sky. Too numb to even cry or shriek out. I must have stood there, the entire afternoon. When Aleemuddin sahib came out, he looked too shocked seeing me standing there. He went on saying—'didn't I tell you to get going. You have already missed so many classes. Why you still standing here. What more you want me to hear from you!'

Before I could say a word, his words more than touched, 'What you said was correct but been trying to run this Centre for years with the little resources we have. Want to give more than two rotis and daal to the children but no money with us. Wanted to start vocational training classes, wanted to get good teachers for English and Hindi but no money to pay their salaries. Doing my best. Let me try more. Keep on trying to at least set up a vocational training centre. Now get going otherwise you will miss the lunch.'

What a relief! I ate extra because of the tension off my head!

20 December—10 p.m.
Don't know how to explain the shock I got when Qamar and Samar came running right inside the classroom to say maulvi Aleemuddin was calling me. He was not in his office, but with a person sitting on the outer stretch.

Now what! What new musibat! I'd thought it was all settled. I had accepted this place as my abode or refuge.

Imagine the shock I got to see Musarrat mia sitting there with maulvi Aleemuddin. For seconds I thought that Aleemuddin must have spoken to him and told him about my rudeness and then must have asked him to get me back. Before I could say a word, Musarrat did so. He had sold off all his lands and given the money to Aleemuddin to open a vocational training centre here at this Centre. Right now he was driving to help out Hyderi sahiba . . . he didn't give any of the details nor did I ask. He wanted to take me along for five or six days, provided Aleemuddin sahib gave permission. Which he did.

So I have to go tomorrow and get back after a few days.

25 December—10 p.m.
Though the very next afternoon I'd reached Hyderi sahiba's haveli, but couldn't get to write before because Hyderi sahiba looked so changed. Painful for me to see her so changed in these weeks. Oh yes, gone her

composure after the hell she's been through. I had no idea of the hell heaped on her, till on the way Musarrat kept detailing that because of the calls she was getting from Lahore—her husband's nephew's calls— the police came to her haveli, even taking her to the thana to question her. Though they let her off, she's been shaken. Doesn't want to live in her haveli. Imagine, such a thing happening to her!

We have been here for the last four days and she's been sorting out her books.

Brought out a lovely illustrated book on Lalla Arifa. She's been reading it. Then another book on the sufis of the Valley. Musarrat mia looks very bored by her constant readings, but I am not. How I wish mother and father and Gulzar were here.

Can't say what will she do with her haveli or with her life. Though she's been talking aloud her fears—maybe the Hindutva brigades lurking around want to grab this haveli and all these phone calls from Pakistan is only an excuse. After saying all this, she started talking about her son—if he was alive he would have been fighting them or maybe not, as the police could have arrested him under any of the charges, under those new laws.

She was giving me many books to read and carry them with me if I want.

I took only four books. Will give them to my mother and father when I go back to my Kashmir. Insha Allah, I will go back, some day.

This morning, another shocking incident happened here—today on Christmas, Hindutva goons attacked a church in a nearby village. Hyderi sahiba got to know of this from Mrs. Brown, who runs a missionary school here and she had invited Hyderi sahiba and us for Christmas lunch but it had to be cancelled as all of them, Christians, had rushed to the church.

Hyderi sahiba was telling Raaesan to make as many parathas as her hands can possibly roll out and also to make aloo subzi and then she will ask Musarrat to carry all that food stuff for Mrs. Brown's family.

I wanted to go along but she didn't allow—told me that there'd be police and netas, who could ask questions about me.

30 December

Returning tomorrow morning. This time I want to go far away from this haveli as Hyderi sahiba is looking very tense all the time. She is so very scared of the police that she cut off the landline telephone lines or wires!

Don't know what she'll do with her haveli. She looks very rattled. But she's in no mood to sell it to any of her neighbours. She doesn't like them one bit.

Musarrat mia was telling her to give it all up to some orphanage.

Maybe donate it to Aleemuddin's Centre. She looked okay about it and told him that she would like to think about it. Then in the same breath added that yes, if he does open some sort of a training centre for the boys.

24 January—10 p.m.

Two days back, I overheard maulvi Aleemuddin telling the other maulvis that many sarkari men had come to his office— to see registers and also to say that on 26 January, the children have to hold a parade and to hoist the flag. He told them that he had been doing so for many years. They asked him to send them videos of the ceremonies they host. They were also asking the biodatas of the children, as they preparing a list of 'foreigners', but he kept telling them that all the children are from very poor homes and most of them from rural places so what biodatas!

Aleemuddin was looking so very helpless. He kept telling the small assembly gathered around him that the money he'd kept aside for buying sewing machines and sports equipment for the students will have to go in the making of videos but what to do! I also heard him mutter that these Hindutva men were looking for an excuse to shut this Centre. He kept looking so very worried.

26 January—6 p.m.

The Republic Day passed away peacefully, but maulvi Aleemuddin had got two videographers. We were made to sing all possible patriotic songs. He had even hired a singing master. Also two P.T. sirs to help us march around the place.

Five or six children couldn't even lift their legs, couldn't march. . . the sirs were discussing, this was because of weakness and weak bones. Then maulvi Aleemuddin was advised by the two sirs to have a doctor's certificate made for these boys couldn't march—to say that they are actually unwell and so couldn't take part in the parade. He called the same doctor sahib where we packed off for the Quran Khwani, for the certificates be made—he would give him the children's name and age and other details but that doctor wanted him to carry the children to his clinic and only after examining them he would give out any certificate. And this time he wouldn't be able to send his van—it's been sent to for some top minister's daughter's wedding.

I don't know what happened on the doctor front—no further talks on this and probably in future, no children would be sent from here to his home. But then, there would be dozens of such madrasas, where dozens of children would be sent for Quran Khwanis.

I think that PT sirs had finally made those certificates. Don't know, can't say at what cost!

1 February
It would be the end our bitter cold winter in my Kashmir—end of the Chilai Kalan—but here it's still very cold. Though now I feel somewhat okay here. I would have been feeling better if the studies were done in the way they were done in my Kashmir school—classes on Maths, English, Urdu. I think Aleemuddin had arranged for Maths and English teachers from some nearby place but they wanted three thousand rupees salary and not one thousand!

Don't feel like writing anything. Going to climb these trees with Shaaz.

Last evening we climbed that big Neem tree. I sat there for one hour, watching those living across the road. Kept seeing the children laughing and talking in that carefree way. They all are living in the pucca houses across the road. They didn't look worried about their future. When I told this to Shaaz, he told me that they had no reason to worry as it was their Hindu sarkar!

How did he know that they were Hindus?

He looked at me as though I was some idiot, 'You so silly! Can't you see them wearing frocks and putting those bindis, and there those boys with big red tikas. All Hindu children. They don't have to live in constant fear like we do! They can laugh, we can't.'

And I, as a Kashmiri, have to live here in more than fear. Constant sort of insecurity.

Allah mia, what are you doing to me . . . to us . . . where are you, Allah mia!

1 March—11 p.m.
Writing after a month. These boys started making fun of me because I used to stand near the boundary wall or climb the Amrood, Aam, and Neem trees, staring so much at those children living across the road.

Maulvis scolded me—police would slap cases on me for staring at 'Hindu girls!'

Imagine, we can't even look beyond the set boundaries. I wanted to rebel and keep on staring. More so, because they were also staring back. One girl with a red shirt on her, even smiled at me. And one day she even shrieked hello to me! She'd been smiling . . . smiling so much.

It's then that Aleemuddin dragged me inside his office and right in front of Shaaz, gave two slaps on my back. Though I'd seen slaps landing on several boys, this was the first time I was slapped. And then he went about yelling that the new rulers of the state had formed groups of goondas to kill any Muslim boy seeing a Hindu girl. He had gone on and on. Hearing the hungama taking place, the cook also walked in, adding his own inputs but Aleemuddin wouldn't hear a word from him. Saying rather too emphatically he knows best how to handle the situation.

Yes, I was really scared when he told me that how two Muslim boys of the nearby basti were lynched only because they asked one Hindu girl for her phone number . . . that was enough to get killed!

When I wanted to say that in my Kashmir we were free to look at the tourists coming there, from all countries, I got another tight slap. He kept telling me to understand that here Muslims get lynched for nothing at all!

5 March—10 p.m.
Two days back, two nephews of Aleemuddin came. His sister's sons. They here from some village near Bulandshahr, looking for work. Kept telling us the conditions of their home.

They went out in the morning .Got back late evening and then sat looking so very upset. No work. No employment. They kept saying they ready to even sweep and clean and mop floors, but even that not getting them anywhere near employment.

They had to get back to their village today afternoon but maulvi sahib stopped them, saying that he will ask hakeem sahib if he could employ them in his home or office.

In the evening, hakeem sahib came and told them that he has himself been trying to get some employment for his own three sons. Nothing at all!

Hakeem sahib went on to tell them that in his village in Bahraich, three kisans (farmers) hung themselves and one weaver family found dead because they had nothing to eat for many days!

The boys sat back, worry lines across their faces. Looked so aged, although they are only in their teens or early twenties.

9 March—6 p.m.

These maulvis who arrived here early morning from Ajmer are looking so very confident. Poor Aleemuddin sahib looked so speechless in front of them.

In the afternoon, they told us the great significance to the Ajmer dargah. It was a different sort of talk and I liked it—Khwaja Moinuddin Chishti had reached Hindustan when he was in his middle age but stayed on till his last years. They said that he was born in East Persia around 533 Hijri (1138–1139 A.D.) and lost his parents at an early stage. Though he had inherited an orchard and a windmill, no sooner he had come in contact with a dervesh sufi, Ebrahim Qandoosi, he gave up all worldly belongings and travelled towards Samarkand and Bukhara. From there, he travelled to Mecca and Medina, and it is while he was there that he'd decided to travel further. And travelled all the ways towards the plains of Rajasthan. He'd settled down at a hillock in Ajmer, close to the Ana Sagar lake. He was loved by the local people and also by the rajas and maharajas of that period, as he was pious and simple and blessed all, the rich and the mighty and also the downtrodden and needy. Even kings and emperors came for his blessings. And at that time, Ajmer was ruled by the Rajput king Prithvi Raj Chauhan.

But when I wanted to tell them about the sufis of my Kashmir, who also came from Central Asia and Iran and Iraq, I was made to sit all too quiet and shut .Just listen to them.

Only the maulvis went on talking, but not us, the students.

My mood is quite off.

I should have been allowed to talk about my sufis of my Kashmir.

After all, they also travelled all the way to reach our Kashmir.

I'm going to try and talk about them in one of the classes.

10 March—11 a.m.

Today saw maulvi Aleemuddin crying while saying his nimaz.

Usually he offers nimaz in the hall, but today he was saying in the garden patch. He was all alone and when I went that side to pluck some Guava leaves as Sultan has been coughing the entire night, I saw tears trickling down his face. I stood there till he got up from the prayer mat.

Before I could ask him a thing, he told me that today is his daughter Saira's birthday. He kept saying it's her 'Saal Girah', and he's been missing her a lot . . . he wanted to wish her but there's no mobile phone with his family.

She stays in the village with his wife. Yes, only the two of them, as his son got killed in the police firing in the dangas that followed the Babri mosque destruction.

I wanted to ask him more, but he didn't seem in that mood to talk.

He looked sad and lost.

In the evening when we were sitting around, I went up to him with the excuse of asking him which duas are good to be recited in the evening but gave him one freshly plucked rose for his daughter's birthday. He looked so happy. Can't tell you how very happy he looked. And he hugged me, patted my head, saying, 'Allah tumhai salamat rakhai!' (may Allah keeps you all okay and well.)

30 March

Already becoming rather too warm. Several days before Holi, we were made to sit tight—not that before Holi we could venture out too much. Only the older boys could walk to the local market shops selling pens, pencils, books and registers. The cook would also walk down almost every other day till the local market, but a week before Holi, all that was halted as maulvi sahib said that there were news reports in the Urdu akhbars of colour getting thrown at Muslims going for the nimaz to the local mosques.

10 April—10 p.m.

An old maulvi sahib has come to stay here for his treatment. I think he's from maulvi Aleemuddin's village and keeps talking of his two heart attacks and what all going wrong with his health.

He talking the whole day to these maulvis and even to us. Talks about politics and about the community too. Talks very fast, couldn't even understand what he's been talking of Brelvis and Deobandis and what all infighting been going on between the two Muslim groups.

I don't like him. And unlike us, he wears only a vest and tehmad, which he calls lungi.

Yesterday afternoon he got snubbed by maulvi Aleemuddin after he gave 'tahveez' to four or five boys and told them to wear it around their neck. When the cook told maulvi sahib about this, he got very cross and told that old fellow to go back to the village.

Don't know whether he will ever go back.

Right now he is sitting at one end of the courtyard. Again, talking of his two heart attacks.

With maulvi sahib telling him that when he called his heart specialist doctor friend if he could be sent there to that doctor's clinic he was told that's not possible, as in the last three hours, three deaths have taken place in that clinic, so the doctor doesn't want a fourth patient to die there!

12 April—8 p.m.
While we were sitting near the Neem trees, with maulvi sahib standing not too far, a family walked towards him.

A middle-aged man, a burqa clad lady, and with them a tall thin boy.

The man kept telling maulvi sahib to keep their son—Hameed—here as the local cops has been pestering him too much, forcing him to become a mukhbir or khabariya (informer) for them.

Though maulvi sahib agreed to keep him, he looked very tense and kept telling the father that no phones and no visitors will be allowed.

Right now Hameed is sitting at the other end of the hall, looking around insecurely. He didn't eat a thing during dinner time. Maulvi sahib tried talking to him, but he wouldn't talk much.

He seems mumbling something. Can't follow what's he saying, but he looks tense.

13 April—9 p.m.
Today morning Hameed been very unwell. Around nimaz time he was crying loudly. Hakeem sahib was called; he told us that he's suffering from no ailment but only tension. We shouldn't trouble him with any questions and queries but to leave him alone. As of now no classes for him. Only sukoon, sukoon, sukoon! Only peace of the mind and soul!

In the evening, I saw him walk around. He walked till the garden and sat under the Amrood trees.

I'm feeling so sad for him.

Shaaz and these other boys don't know a thing about mukhbirs or khabariyas or informers, but I know a little of all this, as my father and mother used to tell us to be very, very careful of strangers talking to us, as Agencies are buying boys to spread or get information or whatever that want.

25 April—5 p.m.

Couldn't write earlier as these days something or the other has been happening.

Two days back, there seemed too much commotion. A woman talking in that high pitched voice.

A woman here and talking like this. So very loudly!

We ran out to see a young woman with two children with her, pleading for shelter and refuge.

When the maulvis were trying to tell her that women were not allowed here, she was telling them that she will get going but only if they could keep her two children here. Her husband picked up by the cops on the 'ilzaam' of stealing cows and now not be found.

Aleemuddin kept saying these days he's not sure who's who . . . don't want the Centre to be attacked.

She sat outside in the garden, with her children crying through the night.

In the morning, the cook gave them something to eat, but she didn't move from there.

There's been so much stress all around.

She sat there with her children for the next two or three days, till hakeem sahib sent them to one of his patients who resides in Lal Bagh— Lucknow's locale for the erstwhile taluqadar families. The hakeem telling the maulvis that the taluqadar family will keep her and her children in their outhouse. Give them food for all possible work. They cannot afford to keep full-fledged cooks; one of those old taluqadar families who though going through tough times still trying to put up facades.

2 May—2 p.m.

Ramzan preparations. Nothing very much. No, nothing like what used to be in our Kashmir home. Father had made sure that there would be eggs in the kitchen and also milk. Gulzar and I wanted to keep all our rozas but father would say that we were too young. Gulzar kept one roza two summers back, and I had kept two rozas but found it very exhausting. And father told me that there is just no compulsion to do anything in Islam, and I should keep all rozas when I grow up.

Here also the maulvis said similar stuff but the cook kept muttering if we boys don't observe roza then hell fires could be getting readied for us in Dozakh!

So should we sit *bhuka-pysaa* the whole day or else wait for the hell fires!

Though most of the older boys were keen to keep the roza, one or two did look worried about how they'd cope without water and food the entire day long. Day after day for 30 long days.

I kept the first roza and by afternoon my head seemed splitting into many parts. I felt very ill and asked maulvi sahib if I could take some medicine but he looked aghast, 'Your roza. No medicines. Just distract yourself—work in the kitchen or help in the washing of the clothes.'

Here I'm sitting in so much pain and there he telling me to do all this! Do this or that!

I miss my family. If I was home in this severe pain, father would have pressed my head and held me tight.

I walked around here and there but the heat was killing. And more than that the sight of Shaaz vomiting whatever little he had eaten at sehri—two or three biscuits dipped in chai.

15 May—10 p.m.
Today evening we all looked very happy when a huge carton arrived from the gurudwara. When we opened it all too excitedly, it was so good to see it full, with dates and lots of Roof Afza sherbet bottles. I can't tell you how much the children smiled and laughed. Several even cried out in delight.

20 May
A strange thing happened last evening—when we were sitting down on the lawns, saying our duas before opening the fast, two young teenaged boys came, carrying two large grass baskets covered with a Hindi newspaper. I recognized them from their clothes—yes, yes, they were the same 'Hindu' boys who'd stared back when I'd stared at them. Maulvi sahib

looked much too rattled but calmed down, as an old man could be also seen nearing—he introduced himself as Thakur Singh and said that he does not want to disturb in our 'ibaadat' but his grandchildren and he were very keen to get some fruit for us to open our *vrat*! Oh yes, there were mangoes and other fruit in those baskets. The man and those boys went back as immediately as they came in. The man adding that he will again come over on Eid, as all his childhood friends were 'Mohammadans' but then went away to the new country.

He told maulvi sahib that his sons don't understand his connect with the Mohammadans, but it is okay for him. He's not thrusting his views on them but perhaps his grandchildren do understand, and that's why helped carry these fruits for us rozedars.

I looked up, towards their balcony. The same girl in that red shirt was standing there. This time she was smiling ... much more than before.

I smiled back as quickly as I could. So that Shaaz doesn't get to see and carry tales and then all this mango-eating fun would be diluted if not snatched away.

28 May—9 p.m.
This month has been tough. Even the days I didn't keep the roza I got very little to eat at lunch time—the cook and the helper fellow were fasting and so were most boys.

It was too hot for the leftovers of the previous night to remain okay, so we made some sort of khichri or boiled rice or dipped biscuits into some concoction called 'sattu' which the maulvis would get from their home villages.

In my Kashmir, recitations of the verses from the Quran could be heard ... echoing and re-echoing. Though my family had very little money, all was saved for the Ramzan month—be it the bagful of walnuts got from our village or the apples and other fruits and vegetables that were dried and kept—either for the winter stretch, or for emergencies in the form of curfews and crackdowns, or for Ramzan, when an additional dish would be placed on our dastarkhwan.

Here loudspeakers banned. Also there is not much to eat. For the iftaar, it would be rotis and rice and one watery dish.

Maulvi sahib told us that in his childhood a variety of fruit and food was taken to the local village mosque. He explained that was because his village used to be full of Musalmaans but Partition took away many—the best possible creamy layer. And then came another tragedy, with the taluqadars either selling their village lands or their lands taken up by the sarkar.

2 June—7 p.m.

Writing very quickly to say that tomorrow I am going for Eid break to Shaaz's home. I wanted to go with him, because all the boys are going somewhere or the other, but I have nowhere to go.

If he had not taken me, then I would have called Musarrat mia if I could be sent to Hyderi sahiba's haveli but haven't heard from them so don't you know about her.

No phone call from home too. Anyway, in these halaats couldn't have even thought of them coming over to meet me or me going there. This is my first Eid in all these years without them. Who will give me Eidi. Maybe no one.

I think before going to Shaaz's home, I'll once again try and stare towards the balcony. Maybe that girl will be there to wish me Eid mubarak. Don't know whether staring that side is really a gunah as maulvi sahib had been shrieking! Too many times all this gunah–vunah thing he's been shrieking! Very, very irritating.

10 p.m.

Had to rather too abruptly stop writing as Shaaz had walked in, came this side, telling me that he is doing so much for me but I have no time to even talk to him.

I had to keep you aside, diary, and listen to his ongoing talks about his home—it has two rooms and a covered veranda, and an aagan and two latrines. How his neighbours don't like them. Yes, yes, he is telling me they don't like his father because his father had opened three meat shops. Then went on to say that now there's only one. Then he told me that he liked one girl—his mamu's daughter and had even told his ammi about that girl, but his ammi told him that it's gunah to think of girls and he shouldn't even whisper this to the father; otherwise, he will have another tension on his head.

He asked me what will I wear for Eid. I have no money nor any means to buy even a topi for my skull. He settled everything by saying that one can get very cheap topis in his mohalla. 'Chikan topis are all made in my mohalla. I'll get you one and one more for your brother. Whenever you take me to your Kashmir, I will gift it to him. You don't even have any picture of your brother. Why?' Yes, I should have carried pictures of my brother but now when I go to Kashmir, I will take Shaaz along with me. His father was here last week to meet maulvi sahib and us and had got along lots of mutton in a cloth bag and was telling the cook that now his meat business has been sliding down as police wallahs extract money from the qasais otherwise threaten to label them as cow smugglers or cow eaters or sellers!

I will try to carry you diary with me. Let's see what I get to eat on Eid at Shaaz's home. Maybe some good dishes before I return here.

What can I give them . . . nothing . . . nothing! But will definitely see if I can spot any Kashmiri in the Eidgah near his home where his father will take us for nimaz. I haven't seen any one from my watan here for so long.

Last Eid, I was home, amongst all our Kashmiris, though when we—father and Gulzar and I—passed those nakaas and police chowkies to visit Shah Hussain and Bahauddin sahibs' homes—we saw those security men coming in way and spoiling all our Eid. They didn't even leave us alone that day. Allah mia, you will have to help us to get rid of those soldiers beating us so much, Allah mia, listen to me.

5

Emotions and Anchorage

6 June—11 p.m.

Couldn't write on Eid day nor the next day as this place—Shaaz home—has been full of their people. So much smell of food and also of sweat.

Though they are kind to me, this place is just too overcrowded. Maybe I'm the one to be blamed—before I came here, the amount of things Shaaz used to tell me about his father's meat shops, his home, his parents' two mobiles, his mohalla, I'd thought it will be some big place.

I'd thought his father would come in a car or van to fetch us for this Eid break, but he came on a borrowed bike. 'This my friend Sharafat's bike. Useless and old, but what to do. Take it from him when have to come this far. Otherwise, in the city, rickshaws or autos.'

All the way to their place here, in this congested locality with broken roads, I kept holding Shaaz's kurta so very tightly that it could have got torn. It was synthetic, so stuck on to him.

Broken lanes and by-lanes, garbage piles. Too much filth. Then when we finally reached the lane where his home is situated, I couldn't really believe that in the narrow filthy lane their home stands. Inside an old fridge, a coloured television set, one takht, an old wooden charpoy for the grandmother, as the others sleep on the matted floor. All too congested.

Men sleep in one part of the house, the women in the other room where the kitchen also stands out—a lot of stainless steel utensils, several degchis, pressure cooker, and that old fridge.

The first night Shaaz and I somehow managed to sleep in the men's section though it was too very tight and cramped—I could feel Shaaz breathing on my head and the snores of the other men were too much. Too irritating.

Forgot to write one very sad thing that took place, minutes before we were starting off from there to here. Let me write these details. Three small boys—think they were younger than me—came running in from

The Diary of Gull Mohammad. Humra Quraishi, Oxford University Press. © Oxford University Press India 2023.
DOI: 10.1093/oso/9789391050269.003.0006

the outer road, towards maulvi Aleemuddin, crying out that they were getting chased by the policemen. They kept crying, saying they were not Bangladeshis nor Rohingyas, but the police asking them for their nationality papers. They have none as their parents have moved to Dilli to work as labourers and they left back with their grandmother who knows nothing at all about papers.

Aleemuddin looked dazed. He kept telling them that if he keeps them at this Centre, then he would himself get arrested or hounded by the cops.

He asked Shaaz's father if he could help out. But he also looked very helpless. Saying that in these terrible times it's impossible to give shelter to anyone, even to little children.

I don't know what happened to those three boys. They looked so very sad and scared. They knew nothing of the factory where their parents worked, saying that their father calls them once in a while and also sends some money through relatives but the mother hasn't called for months—they hadn't even heard her voice.

I felt I was one of them. Been thinking of them.

Will ask maulvi sahib what happened to them, when Shaaz and I get back after a week or so.

11.30 p.m.

I have come to the little breathing space in this home—the courtyard, they call it aagan—don't know how long the tube light flickers here.

Okay, I was writing about my Eid here. All too rushed, couldn't even bathe because the two latrines were full of people—five of their relatives told me that they have come from Barabanki and another lot travelling here from Azamgarh in a tempo. Shaaz's mamu's family coming here in a rickety rickshaw. Too much congestion. Several people from their 'qasai biradari' were also here. . . I'd stood under the Guava trees at one end of the courtyard in hope that the latrines would be less occupied, but no! One person after another in that desperation to relieve themselves.

In the midst of the rush, Shaaz's khala's family arrived from Bhopal. They told us their train was delayed. And then the khalu went on telling everybody in great detail how he had to say his nimaz in the train compartment and what all taunts his co-passengers threw at him. He had to tolerate hearing all that rubbish. In today's mahaul he couldn't even think of reacting.

But even before we could step out and head towards the Eidgah, screams echoed. A crackdown in the mohalla. Announcement of a big curfew to be imposed, so Eid nimaz to be offered inside homes. Everyone looked rattled and tense. Shaaz's father said that this was expected in these Hindutva times!

Though I had witnessed crackdowns in Srinagar's downtown, but why in the interiors of Lucknow! Security forces firing in the air, and yelling at others to get back to their home interiors. Eid nimaz was offered in the courtyard and then most of the older men sat hunched and discussed the political halaats, the mahaul in and around the Avadhi belt. They all looked very upset and gloomy and blamed the Hindutva rulers for treating the community very, very badly. One or two even said that these rulers are worse than the angrez rulers. Shaaz's father kept saying that nobody is azaad today!

I think for the first time in these months I could connect with the Muslims of Uttar Pradesh. I could see and sense traces of that same level of helplessness that my parents and other relatives had experienced back home. Kept thinking of my Kashmir, remembering home. The first time not spending this Eid time with my people.

Along with the others, I said the Eid nimaz in the aagan and then sat inside on the mattress covered with white sheets—called chandnees. Here lots of food was placed—biryani and qorma in big degchis, but I did not want to touch a thing. Though the others were more than eating! The way they were pulling off the flesh and then chewing it was making me feel giddy. Getting on my nerves.

Several of Shaaz's relatives asked about me—who was I and where I have come from? 'Kashmiri . . . wah! A Kashmiri here!' And some of them gave me Eidi too. Shaaz's mamu gave me ten rupees and his khalu another ten and his grandmother twenty rupees.

Salamat Shaikh's brother, Pyare mia, said that he had no money but lots of blessings to give me. He said that after his meat shop was looted, he's all too changed. He keeps on praying and praying. And eats only once a day and that too only one roti dipped in yakhni or daal.

From the very first day here, I noticed one thing about him—in the morning while others were all greeting each other with As-Salaam-Alaikum and Walai-kum-Salaam, he kept saying—Subah-Ka-Salaam!

Subah-Ka-Salaam! Then quietly added that may we all live in peace forever and ever!

Only one or two of his relatives asked about the halaats in my Kashmir. Before I could say word about my Kashmir, they started talking about the halaats in their Uttar Pradesh. Loudest was Shaaz's father, Salamat Shaikh. He was telling them how he inspects each and every animal before taking it inside his slaughter house, as today even a goat gets mistaken for a cow. He had to shut down his one big shop because it was in a so called fashionable locality; he even said that most of the meat was eaten by the non-Muslims of that locality, but they are the ones who cried aloud to shut the gosht shop. He also told them that one minister who sends his sarkari driver to fetch kilos and kilos of mutton does not pay even a rupee. 'Free maal for these harami saalas!' he kept on repeating, looking completely disgusted and angry.

7 June—9 p.m.

They are all watching the television news. Though they have been calling me, it is too hitting and depressing for me to see what all is happening in my Kashmir. Too many of my Kashmiris ruined. Too many killings.

I'd been sitting near Shaaz's grandmother, who was telling me how rich they were before the Partition but now all's going. No, her husband did not want them to shift to the new country, Pakistan, thinking that under Pandit Nehru all Muslims in India would be happy here but all's gone haywire after his demise.

You know what, she looked at me and kept saying that Pandit Nehru sahib was a Kashmiri too. I did not know this.

When she kept praising him and giving him many 'duas'/blessings, I felt very, very happy. One of my Kashmiris getting so much praise.

She patted my back and hugged me.

I told her to visit my Kashmir, and she smiled and told me that once her husband had taken her and their children to Srinagar and then to Pahalgam where they'd stayed in a hotel near the river Lidder. She even remembered attending a wedding there and the wazwan served there.

Shaaz's father neared and told me that wazwan was introduced to the Kashmir region by conqueror Taimur and his men. I couldn't believe all this, but he kept on giving one detail after another—how all those dishes and their recipes were got in there by Taimur. He repeatedly kept saying he knows all about the meat dishes and the kinds of meat—which meat goes into which dish.

He asked his mother if she remembered their visit to Srinagar's dargahs and shrines and mosques.

She kept nodding and then nodded more and more when he reminded her about their visit to the Jami mosque—where the mirwaiz had led the Friday nimaz.

Her eyes shone when he went about telling her and also me that how in those bygone years, Mughal Emperor Aurangzeb had lamented the burning of the Chinar trees growing around that mosque—he knew that the semi burnt mosque could be rebuilt in a year or two but Chinars would take a hundred years to grow.

10.30 p.m.

After they'd switched off the television, they sat discussing the halaats the Muslims in the country are facing. When they'd asked me—I think it was Salamat Shaikh who had asked me—why had the Mufti family formed the government in my Kashmir with the Sanghis? I didn't know what to say. Didn't know too much except I had heard father discuss all this at home, saying that the Sanghis were trying to turn Kashmir into another Palestine . . . how the RSS men will come and take away all our lands and then we Kashmiris will be pushed into the interiors or into the forests. They looked so shocked and kept saying that Muslims have no proper leaders to guide the community.

11 p.m.

Now I have come to the side of the aagan. Feeling very tired. The whole afternoon and the entire evening only and only talks going on. Shaaz's father, the most intelligent in his clan, talks well, knows what's been happening not only here but in other lands as well. He cursing himself as his business is going down every day.

You know what, I am feeling something strange happening to me. Don't know how to describe but strange. The first time when I saw Shaaz's sister Zebunissa, I felt strange, as though I want to touch her arm . . . no, not exactly her arm but something near it. Yes, yes, her chest. Don't know why she keeps covering it with that dupatta. She tries to cover it with that stupid dupatta but it keeps slipping. Don't know why all the women here are putting on dupattas all over their chests and heads. It's so hot, but they go on covering. Why?

How I wish this Zebunissa wasn't covering herself, but each time she bends to offer tea or water, my eyes try to see . . . you know what I'm trying to see . . . her chest.

If Shaaz or his ammi or abbu would come to know of his, they will throw me out of here. It wouldn't bother them whether there's crackdown or curfew outside. They would think I'm turning into some big shaitan! Maulvi Aleemuddin is sure to slap me if he comes to know of my thoughts. The only person to understand would be Musarrat mia, but how can I possibly talk of such things to him or to anyone. Is it okay for us boys to think like this? Let me ask Shaaz the first thing in the morning, but wouldn't he wonder why the hell I'm talking of this useless stuff in his home and all too suddenly?

I will keep shut. Safest not to tell a soul.

My thoughts mine. So let them remain inside me.

8 June—10 a.m.

Strange thoughts hitting. Continuing to hit. Last night saw Zebunissa sitting up on the mat before throwing away her dupatta, plaiting her hair. Her chest not covered, her breasts heaving. I want to touch her. What! All gunah stuff entering my mind. This morning my pyjamas were wet. The latrines were as usual occupied, so pretended I dropped water all over my kurta and that's why some of those drops came trickling downwards. Just dreading to face any one of them.

Two days more to be here and then we go back to that Centre. In a way good, but I'll miss this place.

11 p.m.

In the evening, the family and all the relatives sat around. This time, after the initial days, they looked extremely perturbed and upset with curfew. Some of them talking of the 'Partitioning' times, though this time around they had nowhere to shift. 'In 1947 there was a new country to go to but now nowhere to go, feel like refugees on our own ancestral lands. By next year these rulers will hound us from here, grab our lands, homes, and make us sit in some refugee camp. See what they have done in Muzaffarnagar!'

I tried to see if I could spot Zebunissa. And to my shock saw her peering from the chick/bamboo screen. Yes, yes, she too was looking towards me. Our eyes met but before that her mamu's children came and stood right there. I tried to push them aside, but by then Shaaz called out to her, to get chai and also water for those silly relatives of his. Then Shaaz came close and told me that after two days they will be back to those maulvis in that useless Centre. We laughed.

Zebunissa looked about very self-conscious as she entered the room with that plastic tray with tiny cups of chai. She offered those chai cups to everyone except to me and Shaaz, and when he complained, she mumbled something and ran out. Came back in the next two or three minutes with two large cups overflowing with chai. Whilst placing them in front of us she looked the other way. Not wanting our eyes to meet.

I want to talk to her, but I know it's impossible.

9 June—11 a.m.

Again my shalwar wet. All through the night wanted to put my hands right inside . . . strange sort of urge! What strange thoughts hitting me. Okay, now I can somewhat connect to what I'd seen that big tall boy, Hameed, doing. Once I saw him putting his hands in his shalwar while he was sitting at one end of the madrasa hall. And when I'd told him that I would complain to maulvi Aleemuddin, he had pleaded that I shouldn't do so. Silly fellow told me that red ants were biting him in there, and that's why he was scratching himself up there!

In a way it's good that tomorrow Shaaz and I have to get back because if I stayed here any longer I would have tried to speak to Zebunissa, although I don't know where would be the space to even speak out a word. Don't want to keep looking her side for then something happens to me. Good it's so very crowded here. Can't blame these people here—they are also looking very impatient to get back to their homes, but the curfew is stretching on. Overheard Shaaz's khalu saying that they have to get back somehow as their dukaan cannot be kept locked for so many days. Then his mamu also waiting for 'curfew mai dheel' when he can get back to this Aminabad mohalla. And Zebunissa's saheli is also looking very tense, saying that her mohalla on the other side of the Gomti so she can't even send someone to inform her people.

Don't know what else to write. When I see Zebunissa using her ammi's mobile talking here and there I am more than tempted to ask for her mobile number but what's the point. Can't call her from anywhere. Just wish I had a mobile phone with me!

Wanted to write more. Impossible to write in that sukoon sort of way. Been hearing these words here—sukoon, shukriya, absoos. One or two of Shaaz's relatives are shayars. Very strong hitting verses they had recited. Hearing them, Shaaz's father got so charged that he recited Faiz Ahmad Faiz's nazm and you know what, hearing that his old mother came walking from the charpoy and kept hugging him.

Shaaz's ammi and abbu both told me that if we had met last year, they would have given me a mobile as 'Eidi' (Eid gift), but as their business has really suffered in these months, they can't afford to. Shaaz went on to say that he was also supposed to get a new pair of shoes but even that's postponed. I liked the way he kept showing his near-torn sandals to his mother and then wiping the tears trickling down her face. Zebunissa insisted on seeing those sandals, adding that they weren't that bad! She'd then giggled and looked at me in that shy way. She continued looking sideways, trying not to make that direct eye contact.

Oh forgot to say that today their mumani (maternal uncle's wife) made saffron rice for us—zaffrani-pulao for us. No sign of zaffran but only haldi (turmeric) in great abundance. They kept on asking me whether I had seen the saffron/zaffran plants. I told them that it grows in our Pampore, which is situated very close to Srinagar. I told them that our sufi poetess Lalla Arifa had also once lived in Pampore.

So many details they kept asking me, so I sang our Kashmiri folksong for them. Most of them couldn't follow much of it but went on clapping as I sang aloud:

> Like gold art thou gleaming, O saffron flower!
> To thee I devote my all, O saffron flower
> Like a burning lamp post thou look in moon-lit night
> Who hath given thee colour, O saffron flower!
> Who had given thee scent, O saffron flower!
> Just would I give thee a sweet embrace.

Towards Pampor flew away my Love
The saffron flowers confined him in sweet embrace:
O he is there, and ah me, I am here

When, when, O God, would I see his face?
Let us go to Pampor, O maiden
When blooms the saffron,
It makes my heart throb
And steals it, ah me!
Let's go to Pampor, O maiden
When blooms the saffron.

7 p.m.

Feeling rotten. Twice I tried to touch Zebunissa's fingers when she was giving me that overflowing chai cup, but both the times her ammi's voice came through. She calling her, making me all too nervous.

I'm coming back here for the next Eid—that is, after about two and a half months. I told Shaaz I want to come again for the next Eid.

He looked glum. Then in that same glum tone added, 'Hopefully the curfew is lifted by then!'

His father standing hunched not too far, near the two Guava trees heard our conversation and further added, 'I want to move from here to Saudi or Iran or Turkey! What's left here when anytime curfew is imposed and we sit like animals in this heat and dust! As if it's a gunah to be a Muslim here, in my own watan and zameen, getting treated so badly. *Bahut ho gaya hai. Yeh zulm hai!*'

His relatives tried to shut him, saying that he's getting too loud and blatant. He shouldn't forget that police wallahs are roaming outside. Many, many informers too.

When he was saying all this and then getting quietened so very obviously, I was thinking only and only of my Srinagar. Been hearing this sort of conversations in my home and in the homes of my relatives.

Somehow, the same expressions, the same hand gestures, the same sad look on the faces, the same sort of hopelessness spread around.

Strange nah!

11 p.m.

I shouldn't have argued so much with Shaaz's cousin Haseeb who is here from Bhopal for Eid. Don't like him one bit, he goes talking and talking of his some English school in some backyard of his Bhopal.

He is the only child here with a big watch on his wrist and a small mobile phone with him!

It got too much for me when he went on talking about some big lake in his town. I told him to shut up as there's a bigger lake in my Srinagar.

What lake, what lake? He went about smirking.

And when I told him it's called the Dal lake, you know what he said— 'Dal! Must be a very dull lake!'

That got me all too mad. I shrieked, 'In our Kashmiri Dal means a lake. In Tibetan, 'Dal' means 'still'. Crivara calls it 'Dala' and ...'

Shaaz and others collected around us—me and that boy. And then to lessen the stress and tension around, Shaaz's father told us to tell them all about our lakes—all possible details.

He knew none about his Bhopal lake.

I knew a whole lot because toth had made us read all possible details. I think those details are from the two fat books by GMD Sufi. I remember a lot of those details. You know my diary, our Dal lake is so very wide and large, full of greenish-blue water. Now got somewhat filthy, but earlier it was called by many as the big 'lung' of my Srinagar. Not too far from my lake are the beautiful gardens—the Nishat, Shalimar, and Naseem gardens and other important places like the Hazratbal and the University of Kashmir. Our Dal lake houses houseboats, dongas, and shikaras and with that thousands of Kashmiris living in them.

Their eyes went round and round in circles when I told that my Dal lake is made up of many parts—my father had told us that Dal lake has distinct parts. The 'Sona Lank' or the golden isle is in the part known as 'Bod Dal' (meaning large) and the 'Ropa Lank' or the silver isle in the part known as Astawhol, which is the largest sheet of lake water. The corner of the Dal, known as Gagri-Bal, is known for its calm clear waters. Both the isles of the Sona Lank and Ropa Lank are artificial masses of masonry— one 40 and the other 50 yards square—built by the Mughal Emperors . . . Father had also told us that he'd read that many centuries back this lake was a stretch of land—called Vitala-Marg, which was converted into a lake by an ancient Hindu Raja.

10 June—10 p.m.

Morning started off with Pyare mia coming up with his 'Subah-Ka-Salaams' greetings to everyone.

Then he said something offbeat or strange. Uttered and repeatedly uttered that this morning is 'bai-noor!' As though relaying that there's more than amiss today. No noor of the morning! Not a bright cheerful morning.

I did nothing today. My mood has been very off since that argument with that silly boy. Even now, he's been talking about his English medium school and looking at me and saying you Urdu school wallah. You madrasa wallah!

Allah mia, you are not being fair to me. He, a duffer, going to an English medium school and me stuffed into that no-school type of place called the Centre!

I haven't even tried to look at Zebunissa or any of the others. Shaaz tried to tell me that they also hate Haseeb but what can they do—he is their khala's/maternal aunt's son. They can't throw him out right now when there's curfew going on!

Okay let me try to sleep, though I know sleep wouldn't come by easily. I am feeling so rotten.

Allah mia, where are you! Why can't you help me!

What gunah have I done? Why you punishing me so very much!

Saying all my nimaz, reading the Quran Paak so many times!

Not even looking at that Zebunissa although I like her very much.

Allah mia, please be Raheem. Have some mercy on me. Please do let me be okay!

Why can't I also go to an English medium school. I do want to earn, I don't want to sit like this.

11 p.m.

Feeling very restless. My mind been wandering, wondering—What would be my future? Why was toth so certain that I would be better off away from my Kashmir, when there seems no difference between here and there!

6

Another of Those Traumatic Turns!

1 August

Writing after so many days. I'd even forgotten the date and the time. Asked one of the security guards what's the time, the date, and the day.

I'm sitting in a prison or jail or whatever it's called. They say this special one is for teenagers. I'm here for many, many days. Don't know the exact number of days.

Yes, the day I and Shaaz had to get back to our Centre, hell broke out. For Shaaz and his family and also for me.

I am very, very, very angry with my destiny.

What wrong, what gunah, what sin, I've done to go through so much sorrow! No, I have never robbed or stolen or looted or attacked or lied. Never did I ever pick up a stone to hit any of the sipahis in Srinagar. Only here I did look at Shaaz's sister in that loving way but only from far. Why I'm being punished so very badly! Allah mia, that's not fair on your part to treat me like this . . . making me go through so much pain and humiliation.

That night at Shaaz's home, I had slept off as I was completely exhausted. For two or three nights I hadn't slept, worrying thoughts been hovering around. Woke up all too suddenly when I heard loud banging on the iron-gate, the outer darwaza of their home. Of course, by then all were wide awake. And Shaaz and his father were already at the gate.

Strange loud noises and slogans all around—Out with Gaddars. Out with Kashmiri terrorists . . . out . . . will kill . . . will settle you all desh drohis! More and more of these type of slogans. Trying to think hard but can't even remember all the terrible rubbish those creatures were barking out there!

Those humans were looking like dangerous animals, screaming and shouting—'Kashmiri terrorist here. Not informing! Don't you know, any Kashmiri reaching here has to report to the nearest police station. Throw

The Diary of Gull Mohammad. Humra Quraishi, Oxford University Press. © Oxford University Press India 2023. DOI: 10.1093/oso/9789391050269.003.0007

him out. Gaddars! Keeping ISIS agents! You Musalmaans want to destroy our Hindu rashtra by housing Al-Qaeda boys.'

They pounced on me and also on those from Shaaz's clan who were trying to protect me. They dragged me to a police vehicle and then I was thrown into a detention centre.

I remember I was holding my head. I felt it was about to burst open. Many police wallahs came to tell me that they are keeping me in there so that I wasn't lynched by those goons or goondas.

One big police officer asked for my Srinagar address and my father's mobile number. Once or twice he tried the number, but couldn't get through. Then those usual details of how I landed in Lucknow.

Tense and troubled, I started stammering. Kept on stammering. Couldn't speak beyond the initial sentences. Also, I took to inflicting torture on myself. I went pulling my hair in sheer anger. Couldn't control my poor hands and fingers from doing so! Don't know what happened to me. Just couldn't take the strain; the sheer shock of sitting stuffed in there as though I was some murderer or killer or thief. Don't know for what fault!

They kept me there for days and then shifted me here. Though not abused, I'm kept far away from the other boys. Nah, can't spot a single Kashmiri. And the other boys are told to keep away from me as I am a Kashmiri Musalmaan, so could be linked to terror and terrorists!

Got this diary and my other belongings only yesterday. Actually yesterday a new policeman took over charge here, and he asked me if I needed anything till they decide what to do with me!

I told him I want all my belongings from that place where I was studying-staying, and also from Shaaz's home. I want to be sent back home to my Kashmir. If they want they can keep me in any of the Srinagar prisons. I'd be okay with that.

He gave me this notebook and this new pen.

His face did not look harsh. And he didn't shout and scream at me.

Said he was arranging for all my belongings to be sent back to me.

Don't know whether he's a Hindu or a Muslim, but he looked kind. My stammering got somewhat better. I was answering all his questions. You know what, he even patted my back and told me I shouldn't worry too much. He pointed to the sky and said our Creator is up there who takes care of us.

Before leaving my cell, he told me that I could write anything but nothing against the ministers and also nothing against the government.

He also said he's trying to call the maulvis from the place where I was studying-staying, to come here to meet me. He added he has to do this because the register has to have names of visitors and I have had no visitor at all!

I told him I wanted to meet Shaaz and his family, but he looked somewhat unsure. And then told me they would have problems with the local goons if they re-establish contact with a Kashmiri Muslim.

Don't know what did this mean!

I told him I'm proud and happy to be a Kashmiri Muslim boy. I'm not some bomb maker or a stone thrower or what!

I also told him I keep saying my nimaz and talking to my Allah mia, so what wrong can I do.

Good of this police person to do this much meherbani on me. Yes, very, very kind of him to give me this thick diary. Freedom to write and with that keep my mind or head intact! Whatever remains of it!

3 August—3 p.m.

Too much cleaning and too much sweeping going on here since dawn. They were discussing that some big team of foreign persons arriving to see this boys' prison.

Maybe foreigners coming here to see our plight!

I'm feeling hopeless by now. Nothing seems okay.

Around lunchtime, ten or twelve fair-skinned men and women came and were going around.

They stopped where I was sitting, and one of the women came right up to me and you know the very first thing she'd said, 'You look a Kashmiri. I have worked in Kashmir . . . you look Kashmiri. How are you here? Why you looking so very upset? Tell me, why these tears? You are crying!'

I couldn't answer any of her queries. I started stammering, pulling my hair and crying. Crying so much. Couldn't control myself.

All that I could hear was intense discussion around me. This lady was arguing so much with the guards and officers and with the two Indian-looking persons accompanying the team. She kept looking in my direction and talking. I could hear little, but at least once I could hear her telling the persons that she can't see all this inhuman stuff taking place in here. She wants all young boys to be out of here. Out of this cage! She kept on saying all this with so much of authority in her voice.

Before one could realize what was happening, several photographers also came in and started taking my pictures.

The police tried to snatch or throw away their cameras, but couldn't succeed. I think one camera broke but not sure. Maybe a photographer's spectacles broke as he was pushed around.

Don't know what's going to happen now, because though all cars sped way, this lady and one of her colleagues are still around. Seen them seated on the bench outside. From the little window to my cell (which was opened today because of their visit), I could see her looking very agitated. She's been talking in that angry way to someone on her mobile.

While she's been talking, the other woman writing nonstop.

7

Back to Srinagar, only for a Brief While

10 August—10 a.m.

Now I'm writing from the aeroplane. I'm seated next to these two women who had come to the boys' prison. One of them is Alice who spoke and spoke on her mobile, and other lady is Terry. Yes, she's the one who was sitting near her, writing away.

Both are very fair and wearing long dresses. Both from a foreign country. *Gora* women, as the cops called them.

Again forgot all days and time. Right now asked them and when I asked them, they themselves looked too blank. Checked on their phones and told me the exact day and time. Then these two took off discussing how tough it was for them to get me out from that cell. Even now they are only talking of that—they had tried to talk to one big minister, but when he declined to take their calls, they contacted some big organization for Child Rights in America and its chairperson spoke to many ministers and officials. Only then I was out of that cage!

Don't know why I was thrown in there? Only because I am a Kashmiri Muslim!

They are saying it's going to be a long flight because they could not get a direct flight, but the one that goes via New Delhi and Jammu. Let me try asking them why I was thrown into that prison. I am not a thief or a chor or a badmaash or a terrorist or a militant! Never in my life ever clutched a stone in my hand. Only a pen! Even now this pen is in my hand!

I was so keen to visit Shaaz family and also to say khudahafiz to maulvi Aleemuddin, but they kept telling me that I shouldn't even think of doing so, as it will endanger their lives. Shaaz's poor father must've gone through so much of stress and interrogation because of keeping me with them.

What does all this mean! What is wrong with me! What is wrong with my family—my father so learned, my mother so mild, my poor brother

The Diary of Gull Mohammad. Humra Quraishi, Oxford University Press. © Oxford University Press India 2023.
DOI: 10.1093/oso/9789391050269.003.0008

can't even see very properly because of the pellets fired around. Yet we didn't complain!

When I told Alice that we hadn't even complained about the hardships we were going through, she looked at me and shrugged, saying, 'Complain to whom! After all, the rulers are turning tormentors . . . so no relief from the state unleashed terror.'

She told me she had worked for many years in Kashmir with the 'medical healers', which is a doctors' forum, and knows what all goes on.

She even told me I should consider myself lucky that I'm left alive as she has seen even eight-year-olds shot at and their bodies thrown away by 'unknown killers'!

10 August—11 a.m.
We are still inside the aircraft. These two women walking inside. I think nobody is allowed to get out even to pee. Saw these two women walk towards the washroom. Here they don't call it latrine but only washroom— They told me all this, while asking me if I wanted to go and relieve myself. At first I couldn't understand what they meant but then understood, when they pointed in that direction at the end of the aircraft where two or three children were seen standing with their mothers.

I shook my head. Instead, took hold of this opportunity to ask Alice what I'd been very keen to ask but couldn't really, because the last one day—when they got me out of the prison cell and took me to the hotel where they were putting up—she and her team members were either talking to the police or lawyers or camera persons in that charged way or else talking hurriedly amongst themselves. Somehow now I mustered enough confidence and courage to ask her—why I was thrown in there, in that prison or detention place or jail or whatever they'd called it, and why of all the other boys only I was rescued and taken out. At first she looked all too sad and then told me that she worked for the well-being cum rights of the young and had taken permission to visit all the places where teenagers were detained and imprisoned. The conditions so shocking that at first she and colleagues couldn't believe what they were seeing. About me, Alice told me there were no charges at all! 'Except that you're a Kashmiri Muslim and so could at some stage become a militant! So very bizarre! We called many press persons. And you know they put your photograph on the front page. I showed you. . . your photograph all over. And you wanted to get back home. We unable to get through to your father on the number you gave us, so taking you right there!'

Though lots of toffees are being offered to me, but don't want to touch a thing. More than nervous, how mother, father, and Gulzar would react when they see me. Don't know what lies ahead!

Just now I picked up two toffees. No, not for myself, but for Gulzar. He loves sweets and toffees. I wanted to pick up another two for him but nah, it might look I'm getting all too greedy.

These ladies are telling me to stop writing and put on the seat belt as we are flying. The aircraft taking us towards Srinagar. My home!

16 August—4 p.m.

Been a dull cloudy day. Too cloudy all these five days I have been in Srinagar.

Where to start . . . where to begin . . . all too traumatic. What all to say, what all to write!

Right from the airport, all I could see were security men all over my Kashmir. Less of my Kashmiris and more of these men with rifles and big guns in their hands and also pistols tied to their waist. Scary! How dangerous they looked; much more dangerous than what they looked like months back when I used to see them marching near home and near the school and all over our streets, not even sparing our gardens and orchards and meadows.

The taxi man looked subdued and sad even as these women tried asking him about the halaats in the city. When they went on and on, he told them he cannot speak out because how does he know that the two— Alice and Terry—are not from some American and Israeli agencies. That's when Alice took out her card—she calling it—visiting card—and showed it to the young driver but he still wouldn't speak, only muttering, 'All these security people have taken up our place. Why ask me about my place! See how it looks! Don't show me all these cards. Don't trust anyone now. We been cheated and betrayed and now caged! All you Americans and Israelis come here as tourists but do so many other dangerous things!'

Alice and Terry kept telling him not to generalize so much. And that they were here only to drop a child back home. And then they go back after spending some days in a houseboat on the Dal.

He then came up with a shock of sort—he wouldn't be able to drive up to the downtown address—my address these two women had given him—as there's total curfew till there so he could leave us at the Shah-i-Hamadan shrine and from there we walk or do what we want to.

The curfew pass had to be made at some big office. I kept sitting on the back seat of the taxi till Alice called out for me and then after big arguments between her and the issuing officer, with her even showing him many papers tucked in a huge big envelope with her, the passes were made and then flung at her.

The driver braked close to the Jhelum river, much before the lane leading to the shrine. As we walked ahead, I looked around. Maybe I see someone from my neighbourhood but there wasn't a soul around. Don't know why these two women were so keen to visit the interiors of this shrine, when I was dying to visit my home. Terry was telling Alice that she read some big historian Percy Brown's description of this wooden shrine and all those descriptive passages were very much in her head.

The lone caretaker of the shrine kept looking at them as they gazed at the interiors. Their gaze unmoving from the Khatamband ceiling. Nah, they didn't seem one bit self-conscious, kept on and on talking about the architecture of this ziarat, how the wooden architecture reminded them of the chapels atop the Alps mountain ranges—the Austrian chalets, the churches of Scandinavia, the wooden churches (Stavekirke) of Norway of the eleventh to the fourteenth centuries.

The caretaker tried to tell them about the significance to the shrine, but they seemed to know so much. Alice told him that she'd been here several times before and knows all possible details. Terry told him she read Percy Brown in *Indian Architecture* (the Islamic Period) that this particular type of architecture is made out of wood and holds out with sloping roofs rising in tiers, so as to form a kind of pyramid, with gables and overhanging eaves, each surface waterproofed with layers of birch bark. Adding that the similarities in the design and architecture between the wooden structures of these shrines and the chapels of the Alps, is probably because the climatic conditions of Kashmir are similar to that of the European countries.

I was very restless and tense, but their talks wouldn't stop.

I think they finally realized I was getting impatient, but Terry kept saying that she's not sure whether she'll be able to come this side of the Srinagar city, ever again. And unlike Alice, this is her very first visit here. Could be the very last too.

Don't know after how many minutes we walked out of the shrine, with Alice telling me to lead the way to my home. We were stopped at two check posts and each time Alice and Terry showed the passes, with the security person looking more than intrigued—two foreigners and a young Kashmiri boy. All along the short distance, stray dogs barking. No locals around except one pheran clad old woman crying out hysterically in Kashmiri. She was beating her sagging chest, crying aloud, 'All my Pandit friends could leave this place but not I. Know will die in this Indian prison. Why can't I run away from the everyday brutalities! Why can't I fly out like a bird to meet my children living on the other side of the river!'

Alice and Terry asked me to translate what that woman was crying out. And I did. They nodded in that subdued way and walked along.

Mixed emotions hitting as we stopped and stood in front of my home.

I kept standing there, at the closed outer wooden door, even as Alice kept whispering in my quivering ear, that I should knock or call out.

I did none of the two.

Stood there and wept.

While she knocked very, very gently.

I could hear Gulzar's voice—soft as ever. Then came the sound of his feet.

My twin brother there. Yes, standing there.

I wanted to hug him but couldn't. The flow of tears intensified as he looked at me —he looked so frail and weak and his one eye still bandaged.

Behind him stood my father. Aged and wrinkled and looking dazed.

The two women walked in, helped me walk in, into my own home.

Alice told me to explain to my father and brother that I'm finally back, to be with them forever and forever.

I nodded, kept nodding. Sure that mother and grandmother would come running from the kitchen but there wasn't a soul around. I looked for them. And it's then that father and Gulzar clasped me. Held me tight and slowly said that mother is resting.

But mother never rested in the afternoon. She would be in and around the kitchen, either washing the dishes or cooking something or the other.

Gulzar cried out in that nervous sort of way. Father couldn't control him as he kept crying, in between saying that she's now gone to Allah and now resting there in her grave. Grandmother also gone. She too resting in her grave.

Couldn't grasp all this. The entire place seemed dead and before I knew what was happening I fell on the sheets untidily covering the floor of the front room of my home.

Much later in the afternoon, don't know how Gulzar and father helped me walk to the small park near the roundabout to our lane, where several graves had always stood out amidst rose shrubs. Yes, Gulzar and I used to play hide and seek there, around those graves. Now many more graves and not a trace of any of the rose shrubs.

Alice and Terry stood near the graves as I bent down and fell on my mother's freshly made grave. I kept screaming in agony. Kept asking my brother and father who put my mother in there. Who did? My father looked at his hands and then stretched his arms towards nowhere in particular, 'I did. Have now become a grave digger. No shawls to sell. What to do! Now digging graves. At time I get money for the digging, at times nothing. Somehow feeding Gulzar. Imagine me digging graves. Allah!'

By the time we got up to get back to the lane, the place was crowded with security men . . . more and more of them. I did not quite comprehend whether they were there to keep a watch on the two foreign women or on us. They looked stern with guns clutched tight in their hands.

As Alice hugged me and tried telling me that it was time for her and Terry to go, my father looked all too puzzled. He kept asking them to come inside our home. Then with folded hands, he telling the two women to take me back from wherever they had got me, 'What will he do here! He will be destroyed. How many more graves will I have to dig!'

Alice and Terry made Gulzar get some water from the kitchen for my father to sip, but he continued pleading they take me away. Calming him with words and assurances but nothing seemed to work as my father looked nervous and much too anxious.

Alice then tried to drag along distractions; talking about food and chai—asking my father and brother what did they eat during the day or yesterday or the day before yesterday? Did they have lots of meat? Did they drink kehwah?

He and Gulzar looked blank. Probably to make up for that foodless situation, his genius once again came to the fore. He took to reciting one verse after another.

I'm trying to remember the exact words—Once or twice before, I'd heard him saying aloud these lines of Mahmud Gami.

Today again, he recited these lines till Gulzar sat back, as though he'd eaten! Words of Mahmud Gami, if not roasted meat:

I asked of the butcher the meaning of love's art.
He said 'tie thy heart with the fork of Love.
This roasted meat tastes better while burning.

Suddenly Alice asked him and Gulzar to come along with them—they told us that they had booked for themselves some big houseboat at the further end of the Dal lake, and we should also stay there. She kept on assuring and re-assuring my father that it will be safe. She told him she had earlier worked in Kashmir, so she is well aware of the dark ground realities in the Valley. She kept insisting that we also move to the houseboat with them, stay there for the days they'd be in Srinagar.

That's how I'm at this houseboat called 'Badshah Palace'.

Shukar Allah, Shukar Allah!

I am writing all this, sitting here, in this houseboat.

My father and Gulzar and I are staying in one small houseboat, while Alice and Terry staying in a bigger one. The owner, Ghulam Meer, been telling us that earlier he had seven houseboats but now only two remain. He repeated this one sentence over and over again: 'Like we humans even these houseboats are crumbling, need a lot of looking after. Imagine, my sorrow, out of seven, the fleet stands reduced to only two.'

Then he kept chanting Shukar Allah!

16 August—9 p.m.

My father is not talking to me like he used to. Earlier he would keep on chatting. Now, nothing beyond a sentence or two. He is looking so very frail. Now the only time he talks to me is to tell me to get going from here, along with Gulzar. He then begins talking of the bygones—how way back in 1947 his father and grandfather had helped the Indian Army in trying to kill all the invaders and the tribal lot entering our Kashmir but what reward they'd got—today their children and grandchildren are sitting like frightened and hounded refugees in their own Kashmir.

These two women and the houseboat owner Ghulam Meer talked to my father for a very long time, but my father was still looking very restless, as though on the verge of a nervous breakdown. Alice been telling him that she and Terry had to fly back to Dilli, but they have been postponing their return till he feels better, recovers. They also told him that to move out of Srinagar around 15 August could be somewhat difficult, as there would be travel and traffic restrictions and curbs. So they extending their staying by a couple of days.

Alice also been telling the houseboat owner that they are worried about me. Where can they leave me and for how long? They want to check if some good boys' hostels in the Kashmir region, but their phones and laptops are not working. Meer sahib took them to his houseboat office where the landline could be working. He kept saying, 'This is Kashmir, even simple old fashioned phones could get killed!' Then looked around in that insecure sapped way and added, 'You know killed by whom! By unknown killers!'

11 p.m.
Barely had we sat down for dinner—Alice beamed as never before—saying that she had contacted her office via Meer's sahib's landline, to find a school for me and they called back to say they found one in Calicut. Yes, a good safe place.

First, they will take me there and then make suitable arrangements for father and Gulzar to be there.

Of course, father heard and even understood all that was being said, but he asked Meer sahib to repeat what was being said, though took care to add, 'Of course I know English. I know English very well. Been reading books, reading out to my children, teaching them all about our great place, telling them of the writings by the world famous history people. Have been selling our pashmina shawls to the world famous people. But repeat all this. Don't know why but feeling so very tense!'

Then, he said that Gulzar should go with me, but he will never leave his home and his place. He has to tend to mother's grave and be here. He kept saying that mother's grave needs looking after. His worry that all the graves could be destroyed!

17 August—10 a.m.
Tomorrow time to leave—as of now only me, as Gulzar refuses to leave father. Even I don't want to move from here. Don't want to leave Gulzar and father in this condition, but the entire night he kept crying and trying to tell me that if I don't move from here we will all perish. Meer sahib was telling him that he heard from the two women that the place where they

are taking me to is good and very safe. No, no, not one bit like the madrasas but a proper English-medium school with a hostel. So I go and study very hard and take up some work and then look my father and brother.

Maybe what he is saying makes sense.

But I want Gulzar to come along with me. How will my poor brother—with one damaged eye—travel alone.

I can't understand what will happen to his life when there's nothing to eat. Our home kitchen had never looked so bare. I think nothing cooked for days. Yes, Gulzar always looked weak but never his bones sticking out so much. Yes, I could see his chest bones all out. Even father looks twenty years older in these months.

5 p.m.
All through the afternoon we have been sitting in this garden next to the houseboats. Looking out, towards the lone shikara rowing towards that fishermen's village at one end of the Dal lake. The beautiful Zabarwan Range of mountains right in front of the Dal lake, and the Naseem Bagh in the backdrop.

The sound of the water around the houseboats carrying eerie sounds. I kept looking at my brother and father. Don't know when I'd see them again. And, in what condition.

My mother would have been so happy to be here, but she's resting in her kuttcha grave. Imagine, dug by my father with his bare hands!

She must have really missed me so much. Last time, the day I was leaving for Dilli with father, she had taken out the trambee (copper plate) where four persons can eat at one go. From that one trambee—and four of us ate—rice and haaq. The left-overs of that rice and haaq she'd packed for us for the travel ahead to Dilli.

My mother looked so beautiful even when she wore faded clothes and no makeup.

I see Alice and Terry use so much of some sort of a black colour pencil around their eyes, yet they no match for my mother's beauty. What a hard life she led. Now resting forever and forever!

Let me not think of Shaaz and his sister. No, don't want any trouble for them. Because of me, hell for them. This, when their meat business was anyway down, and now don't know what more disasters they had to face.

Terry and Alice been talking to Meer sahib and his caretaker Mohammad Mustafa as he kept showing them albums he got from his office room—photographs of the who's who, who'd stayed in these house-boats. He'd been saying that now all of them gone up there!

Before he could say more, father looked about uneasily, saying he can no longer hear of death and graves. He has seen too many dead in these recent months. He cried out bitterly and held on to Gulzar!

Meer sahib also looked very upset 'Yes, sorrow has consumed each one of us. Deadened us. At least the Pandits found a place to stay in Dilli or Mumbai, but Kashmiri Musalmaans hounded also there.' He also spoke of some Razdan Pandit family, who were his neighbours but now all shifted out. He misses them very much but he can't even think of visiting them as he could be attacked. 'At least our Kashmiri Pandits can live in those big cities but we Kashmiri Muslims can get finished out there. We nowhere to go!'

Father kept putting his hands on Gulzar's ears—as though that would be some sort of a preventive. Halt or stop or prevent those frightening words from reaching Gulzar, who sat all too rattled.

You know then something strange happened. And stranger things kept on happening. As all of them—Alice, Terry, Meer sahib, and Mohammad Mustafa, were looking at the photographs in the albums, my father also looked towards those photographs. With a sudden surprised look spreading out on his face, he pointed to those photographs, saying he's met all of them. 'They'd been buying my shawls . . . me coming here many years back. Yes, yes, met them. That's our Dilip Kumar sahib and that one is American Kissinger sahib and that American movie star who acted in that famous movie called . . . '

Caretaker Mohammad Mustafa neared my father's face and exclaimed that yes, yes, he's recognized my father!

Meer sahib too seemed to have recognized him, adding that my father looks all too changed. Too aged. Adding that the living conditions affect each one of them in Kashmir.

Terry and Alice took a while to react. Asking so much, throwing one query after another at my father about the men and women he'd met here in these houseboats. The caretaker exclaimed that they all had tea, many, many times. With my father coming up with many more details to tea.

He'd been always passionate about tea making. He'd been telling us that when he goes around selling shawls to the foreigners living in the house-boats they make their tea in a different way. It tastes nothing like our kehwah.

Now he looked as though lost in the tea-world of his, with all of them persistently asking him to recite a verse or two on that heady brew.

Suddenly he voice came through like those earlier times, loud and clear, as he hummed this verse—starting off by saying that this verse is of Mulla Hamidullah Hamid, son of Maulvi Himayatullah. Adding that he's the author of Chai-nama, and this verse in response to Zuhuri's Saqi-nama. Also, adding this one-liner, 'Zuhuri probably never knew of tea that is why he was absorbed in wine !' :

Give me tea, O Saqi, let there be no delay;
Let me have it bitter, if milk and sugar are not to hand
Had Jamshid taken a draught from this pot,
His slow-beating pulse would have run like a deer.
Didst thou notice the boiling kettle of tea cries *baqq baqq*.
Verily thou wouldst say it is Mansur who is shouting *Ana'l Haqq*.

Terry went on clapping, not stopping till Alice had to hold her hands. Then she said that she'd been planning to write a book on Kashmiri shawls. All too suddenly asking my father about his shawls. If she could buy his shawls and then carry them to America.

Shocked I was to hear him say that now there's not even one shawl with him.

I almost shrieked—but those dozens of unsold shawls lying in the different corners of our home—where are they?

'They all gone ... stolen away ... not even one left!' mumbled my father.

No one spoke for minutes or more.

Till Gulzar's quivering voice came through—all stolen from our home but they can't talk of this otherwise they'll be killed! By unknown killers!

Father sat back holding his head, his hands shaking rather too pathetically.

Alice said she knew who could have robbed my poor father of his shawl treasure—unknown looters but nobody can dare talk about it nor lodge any complaint.

Gulzar neared and whispered in Kashmiri in my ear that after grandmother's sudden death they rushed with her dead body to our village, and on getting back they saw the house stuff all gone and stolen.

Neighbours telling them in hushed whispers that many masked men had entered our home and carried away bags stuffed with our things but father telling us to maintain silence, nothing of this to be mentioned otherwise we will be killed.

Suddenly father burst out with verse after verse of Lalla Arifa:

> Slay first the thieves—desire, lust, and pride;
> Learn thou then to be slave to all,
> Robbers only for a while abide;
> Ever liveth the devoted call,
> All a man's gain here is nothing worth,
> Save when his service shall be his sword;
> Ash from the fire is the sun of birth;
> Gain thou then the Knowledge of the Lord.

Then he put Gulzar on his lap, coming up with another verse. Gulzar also lending his voice to it:

> Think not on the things that are without;
> Fix upon thy inner self thy Thought:
> So shall thou be freed from let or doubt:'
> Precepts these, that my Preceptor taught.
> Dance then, Lalla clothed but by the air:
> Sing then, Lalla, clad but in the sky.
> Air and sky: what garment is more fair?
> 'Cloth', said Custom. Doth that sanctify?

And also this verse of Lalla Arifa:

> Whatsoever thing I do of toil,
> Burdens of completion on me lie;
> Yet unto another falls the spoil
> And gains he the fruit thereof, not I.
> Yet if I toil with no thought of self,
> All my works before the self I lay;
> Setting faith and duty before help.
> Well for me shall be the onward way.

8

Better Times . . . but Not for Too Long!

1 September—10 p.m.

Very okay place . . . this Calicut orphanage. But we, I mean all the boys here, are told not to call it orphanage. Instead a home . . . our home or my home!

No, no, this place is nothing like any of the madrasas. Though Islamic studies classes are on but optional. Many students telling me that they are Christians and also several saying they are Hindus but all okay here. Big relief!

Nobody looks scared. Nobody asked me any useless questions when I told them about my Kashmir, my home, my parents, and my brother. No, I didn't have to say that I'm Pahari or any such silly lie! I think they are not scared of Kashmiris.

But I have noticed that almost all the boys stare at me, as though I'm somewhat different. Yes, I eat differently and even speak differently. One think is sure—I know much more than these other boys.

Food too is okay. Getting lots of rice to eat. Though meat is also served here, I'm no longer having meat. Stopped eating any of the fleshy chunks because as I see those big bones, I think of Gulzar's bones sticking out from his back and chest. Of course, I can't say a word of all this to any of the boys here but the first day here when Ibraheem—the boy from Mallapuram—sitting next to me here in class and also during lunch break on the dining table—put a huge mutton piece with a bone sticking out of it—I almost puked. Yes, threw out.

You know what, after that, all the boys glared at me so much. Then the next day, they glared all the more when fish was served. Why? I told them that I'd eaten fish only once in my life; that too when my father had got home our famous trout fish. What trout, what trout, they kept saying. Silly fellows don't know about our special Kashmiri fish. They didn't even know that this type of fish was decades back especially got to our Kashmir

The Diary of Gull Mohammad. Humra Quraishi, Oxford University Press. © Oxford University Press India 2023.
DOI: 10.1093/oso/9789391050269.003.0009

all the way from Vilayat! That far away country what they call United Kingdom.

The same way they glared when zaffran (saffron) rice was served to us on some festive day. I burst out with our saffron song. I didn't want to sing that song, but the words came out. Believe me I didn't want to show off my knowledge but was so happy seeing all that delicious spread. Felt as though saffron has got transported from our Pampore.

I had been singing this song so many times at Shaaz's home, so those words came out so very spontaneously, as though coming out on their own.

You know, Michael and this Ibraheem wanted me to repeat the saffron song. Later, while the other boys stood there staring, giggling at us, we sang:

> Like gold art thou gleaming, O saffron flower!
> To thee I devote my all, O saffron flower!
> Like a burning lamp post thou look in moon-lit night
> Who hath given thee colour, O saffron flower?
> Who had given thee scent, O saffron flower?
> Just would I give thee a sweet embrace.

> Towards Pampor flew away my Love
> The saffron flowers confined him in sweet embrace:
> O he is there, and ah me, I am here

> When, when, O God, would I see his face?
> Let us go to Pampor, O maiden
> When blooms the saffron,
> It makes my heart throb
> And steals it, ah me!
> Let's go to Pampor, O maiden
> When blooms the saffron.

3 September

Don't know when will Gulzar ever reach here. When Alice put me on the aeroplane, she kept consoling, saying she will talk to her office to pay for Gulzar to be sent here and my father could also be here. Maybe the Calicut people will give him some work.

Father's phone coming unreachable. Alice called only once at this place to find out if I was picked up from the airport and brought here safely. She was heading back to her country but kept saying that she will call up very often and if I feel the need then I could ask the school people here to send her a message.

Here, the studies are also okay. English, Maths, Geography, History, and Social Sciences. If I study here, then maybe I will manage to get some work, earn enough to get doctors to heal Gulzar's eye and then I could travel to Lucknow to meet Shaaz and Zebunissa. Maybe their parents permit but maybe they still they sitting too scared of those Hindutva brigades. How can Shaaz's family ever forget what all happened to them, to their home, to their lives because of me staying at their home!

Let me not think too much of all that. Too much sorrow. No, no, not good for me. If I fall ill who will take care of my father and my brother!

5 September—10 p.m.
Teachers' Day. Kept thinking of maulvi Aleemuddin sahib—why we never gave him flowers or sweets or fruits or anything on any of the days?

He was a good gentle person. Did his utmost for the children.

Here Teachers' Day is celebrated in a big way.

On this day, teachers organized a lovely competition for us, the students. We had to write something offbeat and special about our town or city or where we came from.

You know what I wrote on . . . yes, one of those lesser known things to my Kashmir. Everyone knows about our mountains and streams and water falls and about fruits. But nobody knows that many of our sufis' verses are on our foods and fruits. Verses even on our spices!

Only yesterday we got to know the topic of our essay. And then all I did was to go on and on searching for all those verses.

Some of them I remembered, as toth used to recite to us but had forgotten some in-between words or some of those end words. Here, they have a library where I found the two books on my Kashmir—GMD Sufi's 'Kashir: Being a History of Kashmir—From the Earliest Times to Our Own'.

Must tell you that when I saw these two books, I held them so tight as though I have found big treasure. I held them and started crying, as though I was holding on to Kashmir and wouldn't ever let go of it!

The big fat tall librarian, Shameeman Rahman, saw me crying. 'What for?' she asked.

She wouldn't understand. Kashmiris are too emotional. Too attached to our Kashmir.

Got the books issued and been kissing them, each page.

My head been aching and my eyes watering, but I completed my essay in four or five hours. Got these verses from these books.

They will announce the winners only tomorrow in the assembly. At last I am feeling very confident and cool!

I have written down all these verses; very, very, neatly. Will give it to the headmaster for the school magazine they bring out every month.

I think my idea is offbeat and different, as sufis of our Kashmir talk so very passionately about everyday food.

Our patron saint of the Valley—Shaikh Nuruddin's (also called Nund Rishi by the Kashmiri Pandits) this verse:

> The body exposed to the cold river winds blowing,
> Thin porridge and half-boiled vegetable to eat—
> There was a day, O Nasro!
> My spouse lay by my side and a warm blanket to cover us,
> A sumptuous meal and fish to eat—
> There was a day, O Nasro!

Lalla Arifa's verse:

> Patience, my son! is like a golden bowl!
> Being costly, none doth dare purchase it
> Patience my son, is a mixture of salt, pepper, and zira (spice)
> It is bitter to taste, so who will taste it?
> No crop can grow in a sandy desert.
> It is useless to mix butter with bran cakes.
> It is as fruitless to impart spirituality to a dullard
> As it is a waste of time to give candy to an ass.

And not to overlook Habba Khatun's verse:

> I shall bestrew the meadows with flowers for thee
> Come! My lover of flowers!

> Come! Thou, O my darling! Let us collect jessamine
> For none doth return after death.
> I am waiting for thee,
> Come! My lover of flowers.

> Come! my dear come!
> Let us be off to the meadows to collect flowers.
> My beloved is sulking
> And keeping himself in remote regions
> Come! My lover of flowers.

> Come! My dear come! let us go out to collect lettuces
> The people are speaking ill of me,
> But who can alter one's destiny?
> Come! my lover of flowers

> Come, thou, my beloved! Let us go to the river bank
> The whole world is enveloped in deep slumber,
> But I am waiting for a reply from thee!
> Come! My lover of flowers.

This verse of Swami Parmanand, the Sana'i of Kashmir:

> What I have sown in grain I shall reap in ears
> I am tongue tied, alas! Why did I stray off my path of search!
> What to speak of cakes,
> Before the grain was good to flour,
> The mill has stopped.

6 September—10 p.m.
Somewhat happy today. Would have been happier if this badge was given to me in my Kashmir.

In the morning, I was called to the stage and given a badge of honour by the teachers for my essay. One of the teachers asked me that how do I know so much about food and fish. I quickly replied—Miss, by reading and not by eating!

Don't know why all these people think that Kashmiris keep having meat all the time. No way! I remember once long time back when toth took us to the dargah of Sufi Shaikh Dawood in the Batamaloo locality of Srinagar where during the annual Urs only cottage cheese, radish, eggs, and turnip are served; he had repeated hundred times that no meat dish is to be carried by us. No, no meat of any kind is served there in that dargah. He also said that if a devotee wants to offer chicken or mutton as part of his mannat (fulfilment of a wish), then after he'd prayed at the dargah, he can make that offering outside the dargah premises.

7 Septmber—7 p.m.
Spoke to Mobeen and Murshid, the two senior boys, in my hostel, and they were telling me that when they went to give the correction copies to the teachers in the staff room they also saw the news on the television set, kept in that room. All very sad stuff happening in my Kashmir and all that violence spreading to other places as well.

No point asking them too much because I know too well what all must be happening—killings what else!

Let me study as hard as I can. I'm dying to send a message to Alice. I want father and Gulzar to come here before winter cold kills them. You know our harshest winter weeks will start off from mid-December till about January-end. Those forty days get too cold. Can't even describe how very cold.

Here, it will be very warm and enough to eat so they will not fall ill.

10 September—10 p.m.
Got talking to Michael during recess. Don't know why he asked me so much about Lucknow—where I studied there, where I stayed, did I see the Residency. When I asked him what Residency, he even got me a book on it from the library. Lisping— 'Gull, know about other places too, not only and only about your Kashmir!'

Then once again he brought up the topic of Lucknow.

I had to ask him why so much Lucknow? Is he planning to shift there or what!

He told me that busloads are coming from there to here, as too much violence and problems taking place there, so many Muslims shifting here.

Let me ask one of the teachers about all those details. Or let me try read today's newspapers but that will take ages—can do so only after lunchtime or maybe during the sports hour.

Don't know what to do. Been thinking so much about Shaaz and Zebunissa, and their home. They were good to me . . . very good.

Allah mia, can I marry Zebunissa? I really do like her.

If they want I can shift to Lucknow, only for some months or weeks, but will have to get my brother and my father to live with us there.

I can also help them in their meat business. No, no, I hate the sight of raw meaty, fleshy chunks.

I think I will take Zebunissa and Shaaz to my Kashmir, we start some work there. They will love my Kashmir. I will take them to my Gulmarg and Pahalgam and show them all our gardens. They will love it, but then those curfews and crackdowns and what the hell!

11 September

Soon after lunchtime, I read all those details in the newspapers and then saw all of it on that big television set placed in that staff room's corner table.

Without taking any of the permissions from any of the persons here, I rushed out of the gates, towards the bus stand.

Many, many people were either getting off or sitting there stranded. They all looked from Uttar Pradesh and speaking Urdu.

Asked several families whether they have seen Shaaz's family—gave details to their house and the mohalla but they looked blank.

I did not want to ask those three women with prayer beads in their hands, their beady eyes wandering all over. Didn't like the way they were staring all around in that terribly un-nerving curious way.

Ask whom? Everybody looked so tense. Was wondering, when two old men called me to sit and then calmly repeat all those details. Was I looking for someone who'd travelled here from Lucknow?

I did tell them all possible details about Shaaz's family.

They nodded.

And then as calmly as possible told me—that family had been forced to flee from their ancestral home and mohalla and then lynched by unknown killers! As they'd housed a Kashmiri boy!

No, I couldn't believe a word of this.

I somehow picked up the confidence and energy to walk away, towards the small group of young men who had a list of passengers, all those reaching here.

Once again I asked them about Shaaz's family.

They stared at me. And counter asked—'When you looking a Kashmiri, so why so interested in that Uttar Pradesh family?'

Before I could give out any explanations, they repeated what I'd heard a minute back. They made it more than authentic as they told me they are from the same mohalla of downtown Lucknow and saw Salamat sahib's entire family getting hounded out from their home, dragged out by Hindutva goons. Then made to run till they couldn't run any further!

I came running back.

Ibraheem and Michael and the staff had been looking for me.

I told them to leave me alone! Pleaded to be left alone.

Me and my diary.

I can't believe all this. No, none of those details. Nothing going into my head.

What sabr!

Allah mia, where are you!

Allah mia . . . too much! I Want to rest!

Sabr, Sabr, Sabr.

(That evening Gull Mohammad was found slumped, his head on his diary and a pen still clutched in his fingers. As though he was still trying to go on scribbling away Sabr Sabr Sabr—scribbled all over the last page of his diary.)

Index

For the benefit of digital users, indexed terms that span two pages (e.g., 52–53) may, on occasion, appear on only one of those pages.